POETRY EMOTIONS

South East England

Edited by Rob Harding

First published in Great Britain in 2016 by:

 Young**Writers**

Remus House
Coltsfoot Drive
Peterborough
PE2 9BF
Telephone: 01733 890066
Website: www.youngwriters.co.uk
Book Design by Ashley Janson
SB ISBN 978-1-78624-208-2

Printed and bound in the UK by BookPrintingUK
Website: www.bookprintinguk.com

Foreword

Welcome, Reader!

For Young Writers' latest competition, *Poetry Emotions*, we gave school children nationwide the task of writing a poem all about emotions, and they rose to the challenge magnificently!

Pupils could either write about emotions they've felt themselves or create a character to represent an emotion. Which one they chose was entirely up them. Our aspiring poets have also developed their creative skills along the way, getting to grips with poetic techniques such as rhyme, simile and alliteration to bring their thoughts to life. The result is this entertaining collection that allows us a fascinating glimpse into the minds of the next generation, giving us an insight into their innermost feelings. It also makes a great keepsake for years to come.

Here at Young Writers our aim is to encourage creativity in children and to inspire a love of the written word, so it's great to get such an amazing response, with some absolutely fantastic poems. This made it a tough challenge to pick the winners, so well done to *Emily Wood* who has been chosen as the best author in this anthology.

I'd like to congratulate all the young authors in *Poetry Emotions – South East England –* I hope this inspires them to continue with their creative writing.

Jenni Bannister

Editorial Manager

Our charity partner for this academic year is ...

YOUNGMINDS

The voice for young people's **mental health and wellbeing**

We're aiming to raise a huge £5,000 this academic year to help raise awareness for YoungMinds and the great work they do to support children and young people.

If you would like to get involved visit
www.justgiving.com/Young-Writers

YoungMinds is the UK's leading charity committed to improving the emotional wellbeing and mental health of children and young people. They campaign, research and influence policy and practice on behalf of children and young people to improve care and services. They also provide expert knowledge to professionals, parents and young people through the Parents' Helpline, online resources, training and development, outreach work and publications. Their mission is to improve the emotional resilience of all children and to ensure that those who suffer ill mental health get fast and effective support.

www.youngminds.org.uk

Contents

Focus School Hindhead, Hindhead

Knights Enham Junior School, Andover

Moyles Court School Limited, Ringwood

Portsdown Primary School, Portsmouth

St Augustine Of Canterbury RC Primary School, Gillingham

St Cuthbert Mayne Catholic Primary School, Cranleigh

St Lawrence CE Primary School, Sevenoaks

St Mary's & St Peter's CE Primary School, Teddington

St Mary's Catholic Primary School, London

Shoreham Beach Primary School, Shoreham-By-Sea

Wonersh & Shamley Green Primary School, Guildford

The Poems

What Makes Me Happy

The light is fading,
The sun is waving,
I bring the sun back with a fight,
Now the sun is very bright,
The sky is full of delight.

The wind is whistling,
The leaves are trickling,
I dance with the layering texture,
Until there is no noisy mixture,
The sound is full of pleasure.

My friends are stroppy
They're really unhappy,
It doesn't matter if they're girl or boy,
I'll bring them a little toy,
My friends are full of joy.

My words are coming out funny,
And now I'm not feeling very sunny,
I bring my right word back without going mad,
Now I'm feeling not so bad,
My words are really glad.

And finally,
Most definitely,
What will make me happy,
And is not at all tacky,
Is winning the Emotions poetry competition,
Now that's gonna make me really happy.

Plengpailind Suwandee (8)
Albourne CE Primary School, Hassocks

Red Reaction

By far the most irritating thing for me is when my face turns red.
I can't stop this red reaction.
Embarrassment makes me red.
When my dad starts singing, I can feel my cheeks turning scarlet.
I turn red if you make fun of me.
Embarrassed if I arrived at school in fancy dress on the wrong day!
Heat turns me red.
Hot when I look in the mirror at the end of a sunny day on holiday, my face is burnt to a crisp.
Hot in the sun but not as hot as when a jellyfish stung my cheek!
My mouth's on fire when I bite a spicy chilli in Mum's chicken curry. I need water.
Hot when I sweat in football or ballet training.
Fear makes me red.
Fear of being chased by an angry bull with flaming red eyes and a ring in its nose.
The fear of a nightmare where a big, ugly ogre chucks me in a tasty human broth.
Anger makes me red.
My little brother makes me angry; he kicks me, punches me, whacks me!
But nothing makes my blood boil more than being told off by my mum and dad!

Isabelle Handley (8)
Albourne CE Primary School, Hassocks

Anger-Hanger-Ranger

Mum was angry because dad was hangry
Which made my brother annoy my mother.
The next hour I smelt a flower from a big, big tower
It made it worse because that's my curse.

I don't like shouting
It makes me jump,
I don't like bashing,
It makes me a grump.
I don't like avocados,
They make me feel sick
When I am angry,
I try not to hit.

I wanted to call someone because of my anger
She was at home so I actually rang her.

Harrison Waller
Albourne CE Primary School, Hassocks

Proud

My friends are better,
My friends are so good and kind,
They are so skillful.

They are amazing,
They are so funny and good,
They are really good.

I was so surprised,
They are so nice and very fast
And they are so strong.

Lucas Lee (7)
Albourne CE Primary School, Hassocks

Jealousy

Some people say green is for jealousy,
Some people say nasty is for jealousy,
But really they just want to be on top of the rest!
Some people say angry is for jealousy,
Some people say annoyed is for jealousy
But really they just want to be the best!
Some people say ashamed is for jealousy,
Some people say embarrassed is for jealousy,
But really they just want to be you!

Roberta Tite (9)
Albourne CE Primary School, Hassocks

I Was Brave!

I was brave last week,
I was brave as a knight,
I was leaping leaps!
I climbed Mount Everest,
I launched a flag on the top,
I was so, so cold,
I built a snowman on it
I am impressed with myself,
My tummy was saying, 'You can do it!'

Elsa Cutlack (8)
Albourne CE Primary School, Hassocks

The Red Bullet Of Anger

Anger is a red bullet! Once shot, is very hard to control!
This vicious missile may last for a minute,
Where as more bloodthirsty weapons can break your soul.
You're on a sunken ship lost at sea,
With no friends or family!
Anger has a shadow called Guilt.
Slowly, quietly he creeps unseen until his structure is built.
Together this army of emotion
Can destroy even the strongest of devotion!

Daisy Cooper (8)
Albourne CE Primary School, Hassocks

Happy

I was so happy
I jumped up and down like a kangaroo, that has had a lot of sugar.
I was so happy and so was happy hippopotamus called Harry.
He had a huge hamburger and fries.
He hated his hamburger and fries. He had a hammy milkshake.
He had eaten his hamburger and fries also drank his hammy milkshake.
He had a hammy sausage and he liked it.

Ava Brooks (7)
Albourne CE Primary School, Hassocks

Birthday Time

B alloons fly in the sky
I jump up and down like a kangaroo
R ibbons tied up, looking pretty
T eam one and team two are throwing water balloons
H aving a nice time
D addy put us inside
A ll of us are waiting for our parents
Y ay, they are here!

Sofia El-Abd (7)
Albourne CE Primary School, Hassocks

Furious!

I feel the anger bubbling up inside my throat like a volcano.
Up goes my temper as I yell across the street.
'Relax,' says the person transfixed by my voice.
'Impossible!' I shout back at them, fists clenched, I run across, ready to lash out.
Over topples the person as I hurl my fist at their face.
I have knocked them out. I am unleashing my anger onto the world.
Supreme fury!

Oliver King (8)
Albourne CE Primary School, Hassocks

Lovely Books

L ovely books like a love potion,
I ncredible feelings,
B arely can stop reading,
R ather read for my life!
A mazing! Amazing! Books,
R ead! Read! Read!
Y ou! Wow! Books everywhere!

Ben McInnes (8)
Albourne CE Primary School, Hassocks

Scared

There was a great roar like thunder,
Could it be a beast? I wonder
Creak, creak, creak on the floor,
Could it be just next door?
Was I in a haunted house
Or was it just a little mouse?
In the middle of the night
Is not the best time to get a fright.

Freddie Bates (9)
Albourne CE Primary School, Hassocks

Vicious Vase

I was in my house,
Tumbling and tripping,
Stumbling and skipping,
Bumping into the cabinet,
The new vase falling,
Bang!
Phew, I thought,
But that was just bought!

Katie Pope (8)
Albourne CE Primary School, Hassocks

I Am Hungry For Lunch

On Monday I went in the lunch hall,
I saw that everyone's plates were empty,
So I wondered what it was for lunch,
Was it a big burger,
Or some plain pizza,
Or some cheese?
But I wanted to eat all day and not have any single play today.

Sophia Walters (8)
Albourne CE Primary School, Hassocks

Happy

Happy makes me feel joyful
When I am at school I feel happy
When I am with my friends.
Happy makes me feel warm inside.
Happy makes me smile
Happy makes me laugh.

Issy Mason (7)
Albourne CE Primary School, Hassocks

What Makes Me Happy

Cuddling cats, bubbly baths, tech and toys,
I love no noise,
Sunday is fun day,
Library, lunchtime, birthday cake,
Slithery snake.
That's what makes me happy.

Edward Werrett (9)
Albourne CE Primary School, Hassocks

Proud Champion!

I was proud.
I felt proud like Lewis Hamilton
The champion of England
I felt like him.
Win the F1 World Cup like Lewis Hamilton
I'm the champion of F1.

Joshua Watts (7)
Albourne CE Primary School, Hassocks

Loving

L ove it like a Lily.
O n a way to love
V on vam, voom, love is in the room
I t's nice, it's fancy and love is cherished
N ever angry, love is kind
G one in a storm, comes back when it's sunny.

Alice Selkirk (7)
Albourne CE Primary School, Hassocks

Tired

T oo tired to stay, so I go straight home
I need a rest to get some peace
R unning to my bed to have a peaceful little rest
E veryone was waiting at my door for it was my birthday
D addy was trying to wake me up so make sure you stay asleep and rest.

Isabella Daisy Gulmohamed (7)
Albourne CE Primary School, Hassocks

Happy

H ave any sugar you want because I am already as happy as a kangaroo that's eaten sugar.
A ll along I have a happy space
P arties make me really happy
P eople at school make me really happy
Y ou can make me happy!

Natalie Harper (8)
Albourne CE Primary School, Hassocks

Bored

B oredom battling brilliant fun
O n the playground, boredom is a slow alarm clock
R ather be stuck in the hall while everyone's playing with the ball
E verything is staying still
D on't want to go outside, I'd rather be as still as a tree.

Zachary Sweet-Taylor (8)
Albourne CE Primary School, Hassocks

Happy

H appy is great, everybody is happy. Smiles on faces are great
A person like me is happy at football
P eople love being happy, it's a great thing
P eople are happy in places that they like
Y ay! Yay! Yay!

Bailey Sheppard (8)
Albourne CE Primary School, Hassocks

Pride

P utting on my pride shoes
R emembering running and ruining my shoes
I nto the mud mumbling and making mess
D irt on me like a pig
E verybody watching me like a show!

Ruby Light (7)
Albourne CE Primary School, Hassocks

Legoland

I had lots of fun
It was very big inside
I had loads of fun
I was very amused
Amazing rides to go on.

Matilda Rose Lane (8)
Albourne CE Primary School, Hassocks

Happy

H olidays with my family
A way from school
P owerful maths questions
P arking spaces
Y ellow lollies.

Imogen Read
Albourne CE Primary School, Hassocks

My Purrfect Puss

What a wonderful birthday treat,
Four little paws, I couldn't wait to meet.
Tiger cat, you make my heart miss a beat,
I love you so much, even if you prefer to see
what there is outside to eat!

Katie Z Wilson (8)
Albourne CE Primary School, Hassocks

The Tired Morning

As I woke up I started yawning this morning.
I could not even open my eyes and I forward rolled down the stairs!
I scooted to school
I was really worn out and weary.

Jacob Gerhold (7)
Albourne CE Primary School, Hassocks

Always Happy

See me in the field skipping around, with my lollipop in my mouth.
See me in my garden,
See me in the park.
Never see me in my bed.

Antony Paul Richardson (9)
Albourne CE Primary School, Hassocks

Angry

When I am angry I feel a little electric shock
Inside my head feels very warm, worn and tired.
Then I go and have a bubble bath
To rest my head and go to bed.

Troy John Saunders (8)
Albourne CE Primary School, Hassocks

Happiness

Roller skating makes me happy.
Happiness is a ball of glitter.
I whizz around the hall quickly.
Happiness is a warm feeling inside.

Lilly Edwards (7)
Albourne CE Primary School, Hassocks

Dark

I'm in the dark
I'm alone in the wood
It's not like a park
It's cold, icy cold.

Tears are trickling down
Why can't you hear my scream?
I need to go now
Spiders are crawling up my neck.

The wet grass is between my feet
I can hear him, Fear
Gurgling up inside me.

Then the warmth of fire, dewdrops, roses
Springy, spongy marshmallows
Creamy, dreamy chocolates
Makes fear smaller, makes him go
And warmth tingles the tips of my fingers and toes.
I'm filled with hope and joy
A warm beacon guides me, skipping on the path homeward.

Taran Marie Hollmann (11)
Beehive Preparatory School, Ilford

Joy

Joy is a jumping jelly bean, spreading its flavour wherever it goes,
It is a ball of bubblegum, bouncing bountifully everywhere,
Joy is an ecstatic chicken, leaving feathers of happiness everywhere,
It is a bouncing beach ball, bounding like a dog,
Joy is a waving sea, spreading joy all over the world,
It is an eager elephant, trampling footprints of excitement
everywhere,
Joy is a dancing dolphin, jumping joyfully,
It is a carnivorous crocodile, snapping its jaws with joy,
Joy is a frolicking lamb, filled with fun,
It is a rushing rainbow, filling my heart with joy.

Aamina Karim (9)
Beehive Preparatory School, Ilford

Christmas

C hristmas is that time of year for
H appiness and we all cheer
R inging the bell and throwing snowballs
 I ndoors or outdoors, there's always fun
S ometimes you sleep, sometimes you run
T ales and marshmallows and lots of candy
M aybe you might think this is handy
A nyway, Christmas is my favourite time of year
S o that means I will never shed a tear.

Lamiyah Shafique Adam (10)
Beehive Preparatory School, Ilford

I'm So Happy

I'm so happy, so, so happy
A big blue present with a rose-red ribbon.
I'm so happy, so, so happy
It was a card from my great old granny.
I'm so happy, so, so happy
It's a nice sunny day.
I'm so happy, so, so happy
My friend is coming over to play 'Tanki'.

Benjamin Aghaki-Allen (10)
Beehive Preparatory School, Ilford

Silliness

Silliness is a tree jumping up and down
It is like a beach ball flying to the moon.
Silliness is a dictionary getting chopped up
It is like eating raw potatoes
Silliness is a carrot dancing
It is like jumping 21 times
Silliness is dolphin playing Monopoly
It is a shark dancing on the land.

Mikaeel Orr-Deen (10)
Beehive Preparatory School, Ilford

Anger

Anger is a painful pin piercing through your skin, filling
yourself with irritation.
Anger is a fireball exploding, expressing, escalating every second.
It is a red cloud that sits on your head all day long.
Anger is steam driving you absolutely nuts, more and more
appearing in seconds.
It is blood running through your body becoming hotter and hotter.

Myrah Arif (9)
Beehive Preparatory School, Ilford

Anger

Anger is a washing machine, spinning and shaking.
It is the clothes rubbing together like teeth grinding.
Anger is a balloon being blown up until it pops
It is a balloon losing its air.
Anger is a volcano about to erupt
Its fire spreading.
Anger is a tomato growing
It is a tomato exploding in your face.

Alisha Meraj (10)
Beehive Preparatory School, Ilford

Anger

Anger is a washing machine, spinning with rage.
It is a red mess in your face.
Anger is a volcano blowing up in your mind
It is a giant flame coming out of your mouth.
Anger is a tree bashing to the ground
It is a helicopter spinning round and round
Anger is a grill smoking fire
It is a raging steam.

Faaris Malik (10)
Beehive Preparatory School, Ilford

All My Pains

One day I ran a lot, I got a stitch.
Then the next day I rode my bike and fell and scraped my cheek.
Then I went home and I was walking up the stairs.
My sister pushed me down the stairs.
I went to the hospital.
They said I broke my leg.
I'm in pain!

Feroz Malik (11)
Beehive Preparatory School, Ilford

Anger

Anger is a volcano, bursting out with the red bubbles,
trying to bolt and it was unconfined in a different way.
Anger is when your face is like the sizzling, steaming sun.
Anger is when an egg is cracked into the pan quickly
and your face cracks into two pieces,
and the blood crawling and creeping down.
Anger is when your stomach is the temperature gauge
trying to pop up like a balloon.

Kajanantis Skandamoorthy (10)
Beehive Preparatory School, Ilford

Anger

Anger is a feeling of hate and distress
It is a fire raging within.
Anger is a plane crashing from the sky
It is an explosion burning with ashes.
Anger is a banana being split by a mallet
It is foaming like a rabid dog.
Anger is a thirst, a thirst for revenge
It is a fiery, accelerating feeling.

Sulaiman Ahmed (9)
Beehive Preparatory School, Ilford

Excitement

Excitement is a cheetah running as fast as it can in the forest.
Excitement is a dolphin doing its tricks in the deep depths of the sea.
It's a bird twirling and flying up, up in the sky.
Excitement is a wave splashing everywhere with happiness,
It's a rabbit hopping high all around the world with joy.
Excitement is a waterfall whizzing down into the sea.

Zayba Umar (9)
Beehive Preparatory School, Ilford

Fear

Fear is darkness descending down into your head.
It is a person surrounded by darkness, trembling with terror.
Fear is a cat trying to scuttle away from a dog stunned with horror.
It is a light slowly dissolving into pitch pure darkness.
Fear is water frozen in your brain filling it with complete
consternation.

Yash Patel (9)
Beehive Preparatory School, Ilford

The Big Race

Today I lost in the running race.
I am deeply disappointed and angry with myself.
All those weeks of training for nothing.
Everyone's happy with the winners, angry with me.
All I can do now is pick myself up
And train harder and harder for the next race.

Jasraj Hans (11)
Beehive Preparatory School, Ilford

Sadness

Sadness is like a flood, it is drops coming from the sky making puddles.
Sadness is blue paint spurting everywhere
Sadness is tears popping from your eyes
Sadness is water pouring out of a broken pipe
Sadness is clouds crying.

Tiana Gunputh (10)
Beehive Preparatory School, Ilford

Happiness

Happiness is a balloon filled with merriness, joy and cheerfulness.
Happiness is a birthday cake, mouth-watering fun,
It is a firework exploding, fun and joy in every way.
Happiness is a colourful rainbow brightening up with delight and
good spirits.
It is a present filled with enjoyment getting ready to explode.

Caroline Pham (10)
Beehive Preparatory School, Ilford

Excitement

Excitement is a colossal firework bursting out of my frenzied body.
Excitement is a butterfly fluttering around, filling my head with joy.
It is a giant rainbow flooding out of me.
Excitement is a buzzing bee brightening my entire day.
It is an electric wire in my body electrocuting me and making my
nightmares disappear.

Maliha Islam (9)
Beehive Preparatory School, Ilford

Bored Elephant

I am so bored,
I'm roaming around in a tiny enclosure.
They don't let me walk around in some free space.
I get fed up.
I hate it here.
I want to go home
But I can't, that's the thing.
The jingly jungle is where I should live.
I was captured by the animal rescue service.
Like I said before
I want to go home.

Sophie Eliza Buckingham (9)
Edenbridge Primary School, Edenbridge

Sad Penguins

I am a sad penguin trapped in a zoo.
Why do I have to be trapped here?
It's so boring and dull.
I want to go home.
I don't like it here.
Why? Why? Why?
Why do I have to be here?

Abigayle Large (8)
Edenbridge Primary School, Edenbridge

My Only Nephew

I was sitting in my bed, calm and sleeping,
My mum came in and started weeping.
'I just got the most phenomenal phone call,'
When she said that I thought I was gonna fall.
My mum screamed, 'Goodness gracious me,
I can't believe I will be an auntie!'

When the sun lost its therapeutic light,
It gave me a fearful fright.
I ate my fingers as if they were chips,
After I ate them I chomped on my lips.
The sweat poured down my face in a long swerving rivulet.

'Everyone's leaving except for me.
What happens if there is a tragedy?'
I was begging and begging, till my heart was content.
To be a part of the biggest family event.

Everyone came back, mascara running,
I was sitting there, keen and cunning.
They showed me wonderful proud pictures,
Got me cupcakes, different mixtures.
Some pictures sad, some pictures happy,
Some with my nephew in a smelly nappy.

A couple of weeks later I heard my brother's voice.
I had to get up to see, I had no choice.
Outside stood a young man, woman and baby in hand,
I flicked my wrist with an elastic band.
Everyone eating chicken that's fried
As I rock my nephew from side to side.

Nia Brown (10)
Edenbridge Primary School, Edonbridge

27

Sadness

Sadness is like a long journey
And many things can happen
I could get told off
Or I could curl up in a ball and let it all go.

I start to feel unwell
So I go and read a book
I am feeling so unwell
Is it my sadness that is making me feel so ill?

Then I had to go to school
And that would be bad
I ran away from my friends
And that made them feel sad

Suddenly something wet fell down my cheeks
The tears were perfectly formed
Swimming pools under my eyes
My eye is a tap.

I go home and get sent to my room,
I cry and cry and cry until I can cry no more.
I cuddle my teddy in bed
Tears like jewels glisten with sorrow.

Heartbreak roaring through my soul
Sickening anguish consuming my happiness.

Megan King (10)
Edenbridge Primary School, Edenbridge

New Carpet

The bouncing ball goes up and down
Flying around each room in the house.
All three friends leap for the ball
Disaster strikes, the candle jumps.

Silky wax splatters the door and carpet,
We're spinning around; what to do?
Pick up the candle and the ball
Hide them in a rush.

Guilt-ridden friends leave me to sweat
Off I go to bed
With butterflies and a buzzing in my head
Should I tell Mum?

I hear the stairs creak and a voice speaks
I curl up tight into a ball, hiding
A shadow appears in my room
The questions pours on top of me.

'It isn't me, trust me, Mum
I promise it isn't, it was her-he-it!'
My voice is wobbly and croaky
I am scared to tell.

But eventually it just pops out
It isn't that bad after all.

Benny Whittington (11)
Edenbridge Primary School, Edenbridge

My First Tractor

As a ten-year-old,
I bought my first tractor, bright and bold.
Now it's classed with vintage cars
Although it came without spare parts.
Buying my new friend, I was excited as a dog with a bone.
The first thing I did was call my dad on the phone.

Firing up the mighty machine
She sounded amazing, really clean.
As I let off the clutch, she threw a violent shunt
The small giant gave a complaining grunt.

Later that year the winter comes
Eating my breakfast crumbs
Over winter the engine seized
And I wasn't very pleased.

Without my tractor I was alone
The dog didn't have his favourite bone.
Two months later and I was still sad
And Grandad felt really bad.
So I went searching for a ride,
And I got a new one with pride.

I'm now riding with five gears,
Thanks to Grandad, cheers!

Jensen Brown (11)
Edenbridge Primary School, Edenbridge

Headless Turtle

In my family's front room there was a cabinet.
Living there was a glass turtle.
My mum told me not to touch it but it was a tempting turtle.
So one night I lifted him up from the cabinet
I was as excited as a monkey with bananas.

I swung him happily on the floor.
Suddenly, all that was left was his head in my hand.
He called me to repair him, but I did not respond.
I lifted him up and put him back in the cabinet.
My fear tasted like poison.

I ran upstairs into my bedroom
My fear gripped me like a deadly snake.
I was hiding in my bedroom.
Away from trouble.
Moaning Mum came upstairs,
She questioned me like a police officer.
Eventually I confessed.

Dad came to my rescue like Batman to Robin
And superglued the turtle back together
Two weeks later the turtle was headless again.
The glue had failed.

Hayden Sharp (11)
Edenbridge Primary School, Edenbridge

Stunts And Falls

It all began with a stupid stunt,
I sat on the roof of a toy car.
The swing at the ready, to catapult me afar,
My heart in my chest, thumping like a drum.
While a hazy fog blurred my eyesight,
Was this fear?

Forward came the swing,
Smack! The car reared in alarm.
Thump! I was on the floor,
A sea of pain swallowed me!

Out came my dad, alarm displayed upon his face,
My sister looked as if she had seen, the creature of her nightmares.
The colour drained from her cheeks.
While sympathy surged to the surface inside me,
When I saw she'd get into trouble.

Dread churned inside of me like bad porridge,
I went cold all over.
I felt the icy breath of an unseen creature on my neck,
With all my might I mustered
All the courage I could.
'I tripped!'

Hannah Buckingham (11)
Edenbridge Primary School, Edenbridge

An Annoying Penguin

I am a penguin, I wobble too much!
I live in a cave, my friend is annoying.
I squeak too much, my friend hates me.
I am 21, my baby is five years old.
My baby falls over.
I dive quickly, I belly slide.
I like to eat fish.

Ryan Naje Watfa (9)
Edenbridge Primary School, Edenbridge

Hunger

Hunger is orange and tastes eerie,
You just really want to eat.
But it's still not lunch,
I want to eat food!
The power of food can heal you.
There are so many types of puddings like…
Cookies, ice creams and ice lollies!

I can't wait until it's dinner,
I am so hungry!
Buy me a chocolate bar,
Buy me an ice cream bar!
Wait, what is an ice cream bar?
I can't control hunger!
Give me lots and lots of food.
Please, I beg you!
Yes!
It's lunchtime!
Wait, those aren't the right pips.
Since I've written this poem
I've missed lunch!
Nooooo!

Logan Hooton (9)
Edenbridge Primary School, Edenbridge

The Bored Lion

I am a lion.
I am still in a cage.
I am bored of staying in the cage.
I'm not happy with this place.
I can't breathe because it smells.
If you hate me then you shouldn't keep me here.
If I don't like this place you should let me free.
I don't really want to tell you but I brush my hair on my own.

Molly Cross (8)
Edenbridge Primary School, Edenbridge

The Lone Wolf

He is the Iron Giant,
Who stands like a fearsome lion.

His glistening eyes shine,
Off the rich colour of wine.

His footsteps shatter all chances
He roars to stop all happy dances.

The huge giant on the hill
Who stands so very still.

He makes you lose all hope
And makes it hard to cope.

He is the Iron Giant,
The lone wolf on the dark, steep hill.

He casts the spell of the invisible maze
He makes everything look like a dark phase.

He traps you in the thoughts of dark
And he stabs you with some sharp bark.

The darkness is all around me
The sound of him stings me like a bee.

Benas Zalnerauskas (10)
Edenbridge Primary School, Edenbridge

My Dog

She makes me happy.
Every day she follows me around.
At night she sleeps on my bed.
The pink pig is her best friend.
My four-legged friend is my best friend.
She gets muddy outside
And I have to bath her.
I love my pet dog.

Chanel Marie Miles (9)
Edenbridge Primary School, Edenbridge

Innocent Shatters Of Blue

The banging of the front door,
Was a frightening call to open.
As loud footsteps walk in.

Not knowing what to do,
I'm asked to go upstairs,
To pack his bag is like sending away a suitcase of love.

Mum told me not to worry,
It would only get better.
Eating a banana as happy as Larry.
He thought he was going on another holiday adventure.

Feeling guilty about lying to his face,
I picked him up for our last embrace,
My brother and sister arrived just on time,
To say their last goodbye.
Walking bravely out the door,
A sea of tears followed us to the car,
Letting him go with the following words,
'Come and find us when you're older.
I wish the best for you nephew.'
There we lost the happy little boy.

Brooke Williams-Vale (11)
Edenbridge Primary School, Edenbridge

Sadness Causes Badness

S ometimes I feel like there's a grey rain cloud raining over me.
A moment when things don't seem right.
D oing nothing but crying and sobbing.
N othing goes right for me when I have this horrid feeling.
E ven if I try to control it, I can't
S uffering with pain from within me.
S adness is when your heart breaks.

Rebecca Overton (11)
Edenbridge Primary School, Edenbridge

What A Silly Thing To Do

I am Michael, my passion is to climb.
When this urge enters my soul
I lose all control.

It's not my fault, there's no trees around!
I just want to climb, climb and climb . . .

Me and my mates went out one day
To make mischief with mischievous play.
As keen as a eagle I noticed a bike shelter
I locked on like a heat-seeking missile,
I had the urge to climb again.

I walked over, and hopped like a bunny onto it,
My mate climbed with me.
I could hear the bike shelter cry as it gave in.
Bang! It snapped. I jumped into space.
The police were called, I could hear them from miles away. I was scared.
My face turned red. I fled.
The police came, I got given a warning and they left.
What a silly thing to do!

Michael Upcraft (11)
Edenbridge Primary School, Edenbridge

Action Lion

I'm angry and scared.
You horrible hunters tracking me down.

Then I'm waking up in a zoo.
You took my cubs away.

I'm really angry with you.
I'm here with another lion but he's not really a friend.

Now I really am alone,
Please take me to the wild with my cubs.

Ellie Tooth (8)
Edenbridge Primary School, Edenbridge

Angry Penguins

Why do I have to be locked up in this zoo?
Antarctica is my home too.
I miss my friends.
Everyone takes something with them
And it makes a flash.
If you don't want me then you should let me go,
I'm as angry as a hippo.

No one likes me,
I hate them like they hate me.
My friends are in Antarctica.
I bet they miss me.
Don't say anything about them.

Otherwise I'll be upset
And miss them more.
No one cares about me
And I don't care about them.

I'm as black as the night sky
And as white as marshmallows.

Tara Shah (8)
Edenbridge Primary School, Edenbridge

How I Make My Happiness

Sadness is silent screams
Sadness is terrifying dreams
Sadness is confusion that hits me like a train
Sadness is blackness filling my mind.

What makes me happy is my family and friends
What makes me happy is when I am helped through all the twists
and bends.
What makes me happy is the smiling sun.
What makes me happy is my mum
And sometimes it's eating a plum.

Jaeden Wheeler (10)
Edenbridge Primary School, Edenbridge

How You Feel When You Are Happy

Happiness filled the air with excitement,
People's giggles are like contagious smiles,
Every day a door opens to happiness,
Laughter like a melody.

Joy brings happiness to the world.
Sparkling eyes full of smiles.
Smiles lighten up my day with delight
Sunshine fills the sky with joy.

When I fall down excitement hugs me,
There will never be a black hole to sadness.
Day is as lovely as a huge hug,
Positive faces fill people's hearts.

Happy girls and boys are terribly good.
You'll never see a tear when you're happy,
When a door leads to sadness walk around it,
As you step into a room of joy it surrounds me.

Leyla Eyles (11)
Edenbridge Primary School, Edenbridge

Book Feels Angry!

I hate people.
Everyone always gives me an injection.
They write on me and make me messy.
They put things on me.
They kill my best friends – trees.
The people are mean like horrible monsters.
The hot sun burns me.
They totally tore me,
They stick Blu-Tack on me,
I have never had people doing that to me before!

Calvin Eu (8)
Edenbridge Primary School, Edenbridge

Fear

Violently waking in the middle of the gloomy night,
Strangling noises from outside,
Ghostly branches forming into bony hands
Dark, haunted shadows dance on the grey wall
Fear smells like the perfume of death
A black, smokey figure stands like a statue.
Pretty ugly, creepy creatures stand in a corner.
Bloodthirsty noises get louder and louder as they are getting closer
and closer.
I am so scared my heart leaps out of my chest.
Dry screams escape from my cracked throat, the fright coming like
water out of my mouth.
Terror grabbing my soul.
Crazy thoughts thundering in my head.
A taste of blood in my mouth because of biting my lip.
A white and sweaty body
Demons scream all around me.

Izabela Debska (11)
Edenbridge Primary School, Edenbridge

Sad Fox

Why am I sad?
Why? Why? Why?
I like to hunt
Just why am I sad?
I like to chase
I want to know why.

Why am I sad?
Why? Why? Why?
I could chase
But I know I can't.
Why am I sad?
I want to know.

Brooke Lacey (8)
Edenbridge Primary School, Edenbridge

Online Gaming

Invisible friend,
Fingers twitching,
As the Internet gets worse,
My friend is a glitch.

Mum tells me ten more minutes,
The Internet is blocked,
I start to get mad,
Because I have nothing else to do.

My controller isn't working,
I don't know what has happened,
I throw it across the room,
And it makes a very loud boom,
I start to punch the pillows,
I am as mad as a bull,
Then I feel like a fool,
Because I don't know that it'd ran out of battery.

Harvey Sumner (11)
Edenbridge Primary School, Edenbridge

Fear

Waking up in the morning light,
My clammy hands getting hot.
The sweat feels like a raindrop trickling down my hand,
Orange fire blazing in people's soul.

The fright watering out of my mouth,
Dry screams escape from my cracked throat.
A spine-chilling chill runs down my back,
Whilst I'm trembling all day long.

Pale fear smells like a perfume of death,
Crimson blood trickling down the demonic mirror.
Scared fingers shaking silently,
Leaving me feeling stiff and cold.

Michelle Philp (10)
Edenbridge Primary School, Edenbridge

When I'm Hungry

Having food anywhere,
Heating marshmallows on a fire's flare,
Burgers, chips, sweets, anything,
Bringing food to the king.

I don't care who's with me,
I just want to eat, eat, eat,
When I'm hungry I feel like a starving child,
I also scream, shout and make a lot of noise.

When I'm hungry McDonald's invites me to eat,
As it is tempting I run to McDonald's
And meet a long line of hungry children.
Their Coca-Cola bubbles like a water park,
The chips are like the children having fun.
Food to me is like my other sibling,
Food is my world when I'm hungry.

Amy Cross (10)
Edenbridge Primary School, Edenbridge

Happiness Today

When I wake up I feel greater than ever.
I jump out of bed like a feather.
I'm so excited because it's my birthday.
So I shout to my family 'Hooray!'

I run to the long, deep bannister to go downstairs.
When I get down I run to the top-notch chair.
It's almost like I'm in a hall of presents.
My fingers are shaking with excitement.

My heart is beating like a drum.
Eyes are glowing in excitement.
Outside I can see branches swaying like a street dancer.
The beaming sun shines into the house.

Joshua Cambridge (11)
Edenbridge Primary School, Edenbridge

Disgust

Everything around you is truly disgusting like:
When your mum gives you vegetables to eat,
When something's dropped on the floor and you pick it up and eat it,
When someone ruins pizza by putting broccoli on it,
When you've eaten something out of date and it tastes like a bean boozled jelly bean,
When your clothes are laughing at you because you have to wear something you hate,
When you're on 'I'm a Celebrity Get Me Out of Here!' and you have to eat insects.

When you see blood and it makes you shiver like it's bitter.
And when you really see something horrible
Well, you'll just have to deal with it.
Because, like I said
Everything around you is truly disgusting!

Caitlin Gibbs (10)
Edenbridge Primary School, Edenbridge

In The Eyes Of Another

One morning I awoke in the eyes of another,
Trying to cope with all the loneliness and dread that evilly cornered me,
I realised that I am dressed in clothes, drenched in tears.

I curl up in a ball and scream, I am alone, no one to help me, no one who cares,
I feel like an abandoned animal.

I go to school to be battered and torn apart by my 'friends'
They are lions tearing my skin and bones into tears.
I am treated like a piece of dirt, I wish I wasn't here anymore,
I want to go back to my normal life.

Then I go back to my normal life,
Now my only fear is going back to that life of pure fear.

Steven Sapietis (11)
Edenbridge Primary School, Edenbridge

Sad Penguin

I am a penguin as white as suds.
I like to eat succulent tuna, yum-yum.
I live by an iceberg as cold as ice.
I watch my mates splash, I join in.
This zoo is awesome but not now.
I am sad, my enclosure gets smaller every day.
I'm fighting for my life.
My life turns upon me.
Nowhere to go,
Hunters are tracking,
I'm blocked in a corner,
Animals are dying,
Soon it will be me.
Please, I need help.

Callum Stimpson (9)
Edenbridge Primary School, Edenbridge

Rage!

Fists shaking as the Devil fills my body
Anger shaking my shoulders, forcing me to face my rage,
Blood flowing through the door as terror invades my soul,
Snarling lips like a wolf barking hatefully.

Anger filling my body as a rampage bursts out,
Screeches trying to escape my cracked mouth,
Stomping on the ground as my grimacing face fell apart,
Temper fills my body as I start spitting with fury.

Angry tears flood my hateful steaming ears, *banq!*
Fury bursts out as mean as a wolf,
A hateful temper fills my body as my fists shake.
Spitting with fury I run like the wind.

Harvey Roberts (10)
Edenbridge Primary School, Edenbridge

Sadness Comes Out To Play

When you're lonely and no one knows you exist,
When you're stuck out in the pouring rain,
Bullies stomp on your feelings, pushing you right to the ground.

Sorrow kicks you in the heart,
Madness hunts your feelings, causing others' destinies
When you're stuck at home because you're sick.

When you know you have done a good thing
But no one cares and no one pays attention.
I'm glum, low spirit playing inside your mind.
Then someone says I'm sorry for your loss,
Then that sets the depression off.
That's when sadness comes out to play.

Lydia-Maé Faith Hoadley (11)
Edenbridge Primary School, Edenbridge

Feeling

I am soaring to the highest leaves,
With smoke coming out of my mouth,
I am out of my mind,
I am in a state,
I am scared,
I am lonely,
I am annoyed,
I am abused,
I am a fast grower,
I am not a meat eater,
I like drinking water,
I am a fast eater.

Shawn Bedford (9)
Edenbridge Primary School, Edenbridge

My Bedroom

I am annoyed
I am unhappy
I want to come out
I am in a state
I am a mess
I am stuck here
I don't want to stay late
I am a disgrace
I am angry
I am wooden
I've got steps
I wish I could use them.

Ben Horner (9)
Edenbridge Primary School, Edenbridge

Sea

I'm scared when people come to me.
They throw rocks at me
And surf on me and break my back.
All their emotions I get hurt me.

And they treat me like I'm nothing.
Sometimes I get revenge and spoil sandcastles and take waves
But there is someone I like to play with
And that is the sun.

He cheers me up and heats me up.
We entertain people and give them the happiness they need
And the love they need!

Melody Johnson (9)
Edenbridge Primary School, Edenbridge

The Journey

Racing rapidly, my heart leapt out of place
Expressing my rage in quiet chaos.
My skin was lava, burning like the sun.

That's when the explosion began:
I was an erupting volcano, fire flinging itself out of my head!
A rumbling rage bubbled inside of me.

My heart was pounding in my chest, accepting no defeat.
After a while it slowed down, following the rhythm of a steady beat.

The rage has disappeared!
Though I expect it to return soon . . .

Sara Khanom (11)
Edenbridge Primary School, Edenbridge

Fear

Silently waking in the dead of night,
Shadows danced across the darkened walls,
Branches outside forming ghostly patterns,
Strangled screams echo from outside.

My heart leapt out my clammy body,
A hunched up figure sitting in the corner,
Glowing light from their beady eyes now staring at me,
A spine-chilling thought entered my soul.

Bony fingers wrapped around my cold shoulder,
Blood viciously thumping around my head, was it a dream?

Emily May Croft (10)
Edenbridge Primary School, Edenbridge

The Fast Sheep

Hurry up! Hurry up!
Me, a sheep, running?
I could win the cup.
Some of the animals are cunning.
I am so excited.
I'm not that fast.
Before the candle is lit
My leg might go in a cast.
I need to . . .
Win! Win! Win!

Amanda Tillier
Edenbridge Primary School, Edenbridge

Love

Love is when my mum says beautiful things.
Love is like painting a pretty picture.
It's raining love hearts.
Love is shot by Cupid.
Love is represented by Venus.
Love is ruby-red.
Love can't be taken from you.
Love is like looking into a mirror.
Love's birthday is on Valentine's Day.

Olivia Skudder (8)
Edenbridge Primary School, Edenbridge

Love

Love is compassion.
Love can sometimes be nervous but it is a good thing.
Love is caring about people,
You don't run out of love.
It is like you are in your dreams.
Love is kissing you,
It is a red rose.
Love is writing letters,
Love never ends.

Zachary Miles (8)
Edenbridge Primary School, Edenbridge

Joy, Happy

Sitting in a pool of flowers.
Clouds that look like puppies.
Having picnics with friends and family.
Going to the beach and the sun winks at us.
The sound of laughter and the splash of waves,
And looking at the beautiful sights of the bright orange caves.
Children on the swings
Listening to the tennis racket go ping.
Happy is my name and I am yellow with joy.

Ryan Bell (10)
Edenbridge Primary School, Edenbridge

Love

Love is like everything brightening up inside you.
The sound of bells ringing.
Love is the colour of 10 red roses.
Hearts are together forever,
To care about others.
Friendship forever.
It feels gentle.
It feels like joy is inside you.
The fizziest drink is popping up inside you.

Erin Rachael Draper (9)
Edenbridge Primary School, Edenbridge

The Sad Jaguar

I am a jaguar.
I don't know how to swim but I know how to run so fast.
I think my father taught me how to run so fast.
My two-year-old sister is annoying,
She asks me when my friends are coming over.
I don't know when my father is going to teach my sister how to run so fast.
I'm very sad because my mum died ten days ago,
Everyone loved her.

Molly Cross (8)
Edenbridge Primary School, Edenbridge

Untitled

There is no point any more,
I'm alone with this nonsense.
I can't take it any more,
Just let me go!
But they don't, I'm just so frustrated.
Let me go I say, this is just boring.
When are you gonna let me go?
Just leave me alone and take me where I belong,
I just hate this zoo!

Max (9)
Edenbridge Primary School, Edenbridge

Poor, Poor Me

I am a plant.
I am sad.
I am old.
I am not loved.
I am abused.
I am cut by a horrible person.

Poppy Medcraft (9)
Edenbridge Primary School, Edenbridge

Fear

Fear is motionless.
It tastes like a bitter weak salad
And smells musty and damp.
Fear looks like a devastating dark, lonely street.
The sound of enormous echoing footsteps.
Fear makes me shiver.

Annabelle Connolly (8)
Edenbridge Primary School, Edenbridge

Happiness

Happiness is like a volcano erupting.
Happiness is a large emotion, as big as a huge giant.
Happiness takes you two steps further.
Happiness is as colourful as a rainbow.
Happy is what you want to be.
Happy is how you want to make people feel.

Albie Dean Watkins (8)
Edenbridge Primary School, Edenbridge

Joy

Joy is like a firework in the sky.
Joy explodes with excitement.
Happiness pops like a balloon.
Joy blows up with rainbow colours.
Joy comes from the heart.
Joy is like a multicoloured sherbet heart.

Gabriel Lewis King (9)
Edenbridge Primary School, Edenbridge

Love

Love is as red as roses,
Love will always be the same,
Love is not just marriage,
It is trust and friendship,
Love will take you somewhere wonderful.

Christine (8)
Edenbridge Primary School, Edenbridge

Love

Love is as red as roses,
Love will always be the same,
Love is not just marriage,
It is trust and friendship,
Love will take you somewhere wonderful.

Jessica Davidson (8)
Edenbridge Primary School, Edenbridge

Loneliness

Loneliness is pitch-black.
Loneliness is as sad as death.
Loneliness hates Love.
Lousy Loneliness.
Loneliness is as dark as a power cut at midnight.

Matthew Harbour Charman (9)
Edenbridge Primary School, Edenbridge

Upset

All the mean humans use me all day,
But sometimes they snap me,
When you're upset you go all blue,
But then it gets worse and you start to scream,
When that happens you go purple like lavender.

Kaitlyn Shad (8)
Edenbridge Primary School, Edenbridge

Angry Cat

I am a lovely, beautiful cat.
I am a fluffy little animal.
I love a lot of cuddles.
I am really angry when I get picked up.
I am going to scratch them!

Sarah Leppard-Howard (9)
Edenbridge Primary School, Edenbridge

Sadness

Sadness makes me feel blue.
Cold inside like a polar bear.
Sadness is a dark cloud.
It feels like a broken heart.

Lee M B F Smith (8)
Edenbridge Primary School, Edenbridge

Love

Love is the colour of red.
Love hearts are silently falling from the sky.
Love is happiness all over.
Love is pure red like a rose.

Jayden Miles (9)
Edenbridge Primary School, Edenbridge

Photo

Tick-tock! Tick-tock! Ring! Ding!
9am
There is a little photo,
That dances around the room.
Its speed is so immense,
Bing! Bong! Boom!

I wonder how it got here,
It bothers me day to day.
It comes right past my desk,
Get out of the way!

I'll go through the roof,
If I see it again
I'll run out of the room,
But when?

I don't know about you,
But it really bothers me,
Concentration, good work
That's what I like to see.

I'm surprised it's so dusty,
After all it's exercise.
It's all about its strength,
That it will maximise.

It's as trim as lead
Or soft, smooth skin
But it flies so low to the ground
It barely misses the bin.

After all . . .
It is quite splendid,
Seeing all the moods.
The photo is a hawk swooping through the trees,
Flying back to its brood.

Scott James (11)
Focus School Hindhead, Hindhead

Be Happy

Without happiness a day is wasted,
A good night's sleep is always supreme,
even though copy and pasting your homework is easier it gets you
no marks.
Smile your hardest,
Work your socks off
And be *happy*,
Happiness is the key to your life, if you are not happy your hair will go
grey,
A bird's best time is catching their prey,
Wherever you go,
Whatever you feel like
Always give people a
Smile.
But don't forget to be as happy as a cheeky monkey,
Be *happy*
Be cheerful
Be jolly like you've never been before.
Give people a smile
A bigger smile,
An even bigger smile
Just be like a cheeky monkey, and a cheerful bird laughing its head
off.
Don't forget be *happy*
Wherever you go, whatever you feel like,
Smile.

Carling Brooke Ryall (11)
Focus School Hindhead, Hindhead

The Battle Of Emotions

The moon shines sorrowfully on a scene of disaster,
A large, shiny black ship sinking to its doom.
The heartbroken sky has donned her twinkling veil of black,
Whilst mourning for the lives lost in the gloom.

Sad at the lost lives,
Sad at the sorry scene,
Sad at the wistful weeps
Coming from the living.

The sky sits silently in her suit of black,
Her one crescent eye staring frustratingly into the night,
Her millions of ears listen to every tremor,
Every one of her senses make her go into battle like an
undefeatable knight.

Mad at the sincere storm,
Mad at the warrior-like waves,
Mad at the blue sea
Sucking up helpless lives.

The sky in all her glory on these stormy, breathtaking nights,
With two main feelings in her mind,
She's sad for the drowned souls and mad at the storm,
But what she's always wishing is that the sea would be more kind.

Kerenza Marsh (11)
Focus School Hindhead, Hindhead

Going Mad

Mad Murray starts to moan as he has his mad moments.
He starts to miaow and bares his meanest teeth at the stormy clouds
Which gather above the minute Earth . . .
Bang, crash, grrr
Redder and redder in the face he goes until *boom, bang, bop, crash.*
Mad Murray disappears into millions of pieces of ash.

Murray Turner (10)
Focus School Hindhead, Hindhead

Angry!

Harsh hampers hollering,
Like an angry lion,
Ferocious families fight,
Like an angry, crashing wave.

Angry animals,
Are like loud men hollering with rage,
Spouting out of an angry mouth.

Smoke pours out of his ears,
His heart is made of stone,
He stuffs red meat down his throat
Just like an angry red tiger!

He wears red ears like a bull,
Fire seems to come out of his mouth,
Like an erupting volcano!

The moon can hear his anger,
As he is as loud as a fox shouting,
And his footsteps are loud as thunder,
His anger makes him leap at his victim,
His nose nearly explodes,
And his name is called Angry!

Brent Glanfield (10)
Focus School Hindhead, Hindhead

A Mystery Sensation

As I walked into the night there was silence
The moon was still and the world was cold.
I turned to the wind and asked, 'What's happened?'
Then it blew out a breeze and whispered, 'Jack Frost is here.'
Frozen branches of the hawthorn tree gently shook their
sparkling leaves.
I smelt the freshness of the air.
I shivered as the clouds flew by.

Marcelle Lynes (10)
Focus School Hindhead, Hindhead

Sassy Susan Sometimes Sits

Sometimes Susan
Sits on her sofa,
In the middle of May.
Sometimes Susan
Sits on her sofa,
And sassily watches the boats in the bay.
Sometimes Susan
Sits on her sofa,
And sings in a silly way.
Sometimes Susan
Sits on her sofa,
Sassily swinging her legs in a sway.
Sometimes Susan
Sits on her sofa,
Reading a book about clay.
Sometimes Susan
Sits on her sofa,
Sassily thinking about what she could do today.
Today,
Susan,
Sits on her sofa
In a very sassy way.

Roxanne Wickland (11)
Focus School Hindhead, Hindhead

Jealousy

I hope that I am never jealous
Jealous people aren't much fun.
A jealous person's never happy
Or liked by anyone.

If I was jealous
I would be green
And then I'd be as mean as a bean.

If I was jealous
I would want your coat
And then you'd always call me a goat.

If I was jealous
I'd take your bag,
But then you'd think I was an old hag.

If I was jealous
I'd take your money
But then you wouldn't think me sweet as honey.

If I was jealous
I'd take your friend
But then you'd think I'm round the bend.

Royston James (11)
Focus School Hindhead, Hindhead

The Sea And The Wind

I was looking out of the window on the edge of the tall cliff.
The wind was wailing and was rattling the knocker
And there was a continuing crash of the sea.
And then I came back to my senses
Because I was frightened of the loneliness.

I want to go,
I have to go
I was going to go
So I went.

I tried to say goodbye but I had to cry.
I was going out into the big world.
After a while I missed the *crash, crash* of the sea
And I felt emptiness in me.

I want to go back
I had to go back
I was going back
And then I had happiness in me.

Chater Dunn (11)
Focus School Hindhead, Hindhead

Anger's Rage Explodes Grumpiness

Anger rages go up and down to different temperatures
As hot as can be . . . or hotter
As hot as a hot, raged, grumpy toad
Maybe explosive
Or active
Bubbly hot fire getting ready to leap out at you
Or inactive
Sunbathing, watching you with one sneaky eye
Like the sun in the sky with its hotness blazing down on you.

Nathaniel Ford (11)
Focus School Hindhead, Hindhead

Careless

The crafty fox pads downtown, its nose leading it bin to bin
But as the neighbourhood screams and shouts he carries on without
a doubt.
The wind flies past; his invisible body making branches sway
But when he is tired his breeze dies down, he finds his bed amongst
the leaves.
As owls call out into the night, their fascinating wings flash in the
moonlight.
One swoops down carelessly in a world of its own.
It just careless, calm, relaxed, with not a care.
The sun creeps up over the mountain tops, its orange body
awakening.
A new day, its rays wake the birds,
Every animal on the Earth, it seems to say 'I'm careless.'
As the flowers sway their petals they grow and grow.
Every day they have nothing to do just sway carelessly,
Careless as a flower should be.
'Careless, careless, careless, yes I am.'

Magnus Wickland (11)
Focus School Hindhead, Hindhead

The Mysterious Dark

When the dim lights fade away and the darkness swallows
everything,
You will find petrified Penny panicking!
The trees grows legs,
The wind is howling like an owl,
Meanwhile the sunset has disappeared.
But still, what is waiting for petrified Penny?
A slimy, slithery snake waiting for Penny to doze off to sleep,
Terrified, heartbroken, horrified, that is Penny;
Last of all we must say petrified Penny is a panicker!

Charmaine Lien Young (11)
Focus School Hindhead, Hindhead

She Is Shy . . .

She shook at
Bumps and bashes,
She trembled at
Crunches and crashes,
She peeped around doors
With caution -
Would they pounce this time?

Carefully she crept along the corridors,
Slipping and sliding from silent shadows to sleeping shadows.

She was closed up in a web of wonder
She didn't hear the muffled,
Tip-toe, tip-toe, tip-toe, tip-toe
Of a black cat getting ready to pounce.
The 'she' was a mouse,
As shy as a girl amongst the London crowds.
Suddenly the black cat pounced,
She, the mouse, almost jumped out of her skin.

Brontë Blake (11)
Focus School Hindhead, Hindhead

Jealousy And Hatred

Jealousy and Hatred always collide
Be it head on or a mean swipe from the side
A cauldron of stewing emotions remains
In neon-light colours which flash in our brains.

An envious green, brilliant as grass
Colours my mind as I'm left in the past
By a friend who's found a far stronger ally
I'd like to fight back, but with those odds, how can I?

A matador's cloak in glaring red
Stains the angry thoughts in my darkening head
Teasing me, poking me: react with some Force!
Teach that Tempter, on his high horse.

Hatred is cold at times, stubborn – a mule
Dull graphite grey, fights a heartrending duel
Till amber-flamed Fury hisses and fumes
And the belching smoke of Bad Feeling plumes.

Max James (10)
Focus School Hindhead, Hindhead

Jealousy

Jealousy comes in all shapes and sizes
In all walks of life, it is seen
Jealous? Jealous? Have you been?

As jealous as a junkyard watching posh cars cruise by.
Jealous? Jealous? Could you be?

The static stone statue has a view of people walking by so smoothly.
He wishes he could do the same.
Jealous? Jealous? Could you be?

It twists and turns until it comes out
It swishes and churns until it comes out, out, out!
Sometimes it comes out as green as a bad smell.
Sometimes it comes out sassily
Sometimes it comes out with a shout!
Jealous? Jealous? Have you been?

Ayrton Knappett (11)
Focus School Hindhead, Hindhead

I'm . . . Explosive!

I've had a bad day so stay out of my way. I am as:
Explosive as a bomb,
Insane as a mad man,
As hot as the sun,
Dangerous as a snake.
Back off! Back off!
I am enraged.
Destructive,
Angry,
Sad!
Sad!
Sad!
Fffff!

Ronan Dalrymple (10)
Focus School Hindhead, Hindhead

The Blissful Song

Blissful music ringing in my ears,
Blissful times when there are no fears.
Blissful days when the sun is gold
Blissful days when it's never cold.

Blissful nights when the stars shine brightly,
Blissful seas where dolphins dance lightly,
Blissful times when children play,
Blissful times when it's warm all day.

Blissful cotton floating in the sky,
Blissful birds flying way up high.
Blissful, beautiful butterflies flying,
Blissful wind through the trees is sighing.

Brielle Burch (10)
Focus School Hindhead, Hindhead

Loneliness

Lonely in the deep west
As the wind whisks east and west
As cactuses sway side to side,
Side to side,
With their loneliness deep inside.
A cowboy clatters on his horse like burning yeast.
East and west, east and west.
He rides with loneliness at his side.
A bull in a field with siblings, he lies himself on a rock to rest
But left in the west, the deep, dark west
With their loneliness companion to guide the way.
A boy in the west sat in the playground.
Watching everyone play.
His heart beating as if laden with weapons,
Body about to explode
His only friend Loneliness, his only friend at his side.

Lewis John Panter (10)
Knights Enham Junior School, Andover

67

Amazing Anger Everywhere

A nnoyed
N ervous
G rumpy
E nergetic
R evenge

E very day
V anessa makes
E verybody
R eally upset
Y oung people
W atch her
H elping
E verybody get
R evenge on
E ach other.

Daisy Adams (10)
Knights Enham Junior School, Andover

I'm Angry, Just Leave Me Alone

Just leave me alone,
I'm as red as fire,
Please, I want to listen to music,
I mean Redfoo,
You've grounded me,
Now I'm not happy,
Get a bucket because I'm as red as fire,
I said leave me alone,
Leave me alone,
If you don't I'll lock myself in my room
I'll never come out,
So give me my phone back.

Lilly Louise Smith (9)
Knights Enham Junior School, Andover

Sadness

Silly socks, silly songs, silly sadness, think again,
Hideous hills, horrible happiness, think again.

Every day you may think these things,
But you will do this when you're angry,
Your mum, your dad, your granny or grandpa,
Will come and see how you are.

You'll soon find out what I'm talking about,
Just realise,
You'll have a few times like this,
Just remember happiness keeps everyone joyful.

Morgan Jones (9)
Knights Enham Junior School, Andover

An Angry Day

I walked to school with my bag on my back,
As I saw a duck,
It was chasing me,
I was really angry.
As I came to school I threw my bag at my teacher's head,
The terrible teacher was so mad,
She put me in detention for the rest of the week,
When I got out of detention I was so mad,
I threw my bag at my teacher's mum's head,
What will happen next?

Indiana Gravestock (10)
Knights Enham Junior School, Andover

Food, Happy

Sometimes you don't like your food.
It can change your mood,
Sometimes you just say no,
Although you just go,
Run so far away,
Just so you can say yay,
There's a birthday in one day and that's a big hooray,
There's tumbling tomatoes, cutting carrots, caramel cake,
Little lettuce, big burger, bingo buns, and Iceland's ice cream.
Listen to the clocks going tick-tock.

Chanai Allan (10)
Knights Enham Junior School, Andover

Driving Home From Grandma's

I'm driving home from Grandma's
And this is what I see,
My jaw drops down low,
I'm as shocked as I can be,
My eyes are getting bigger,
I think they're going to pop,
This is what happens when I'm very, very shocked.

Amber Woods (10)
Knights Enham Junior School, Andover

When You're Angry

When you're angry it's hard to calm down,
When you're angry no one wants you around,
When you're angry don't harm others,
Because it can hurt them in more than one way.

Jay Sweet (10)
Knights Enham Junior School, Andover

Excitement Is . . .

Excitement is going to my friend's house,
Excitement is seeing my family after school,
Excitement is going to school,
Excitement is seeing my cousins in Newcastle,
Excitement is going on holiday,
Excitement is seeing my Moyles Court friends,
Excitement is going to a restaurant,
Excitement is seeing animals in the zoo,
Excitement is going to the aquarium,
Excitement is seeing my childminder,
Excitement is going to the beach,
Excitement is seeing my grandma,
Excitement is going to a theatre,
Excitement is seeing my nanny,
Excitement is my birthday and Christmas,
Excitement is all around you!

Ross Jefferies (9)
Moyles Court School Limited, Ringwood

Things I Adore

I adore the incredible John Cena because he is strong,
The sea is as blue as the sky,
World's Strongest Man is an excellent sport and is only on at
Christmas,
Acting makes me feel great but sometimes I fail,
My excellent lizard is brilliant at climbing,
I love yummy chocolate when I am allowed it,
Volcanoes are as red as fire,
My amazing dad is brilliant on cars,
Fighting makes me feel elated because I'm good at it,
I admire terrific racing on the TV,
I like fantastic football when a player scores,
Splash down is lovely when you splash,
Tigers are cuddly because they're soft.

Finley Ashford-Ellis (7)
Moyles Court School Limited, Ringwood

Things I Adore

My lovely dad is great when he plays with me,
Singing makes me feel wonderful because I am very good at it,
Daffodils are as yellow as the sun,
I adore brilliant dogs when they bark loudly,
I love my adorable mum because she reads me stories,
India is my best friend and she plays with me,
Puppies are terrific when they play with me,
My little pig is terrific when he wriggles his bottom,
Reading makes me feel great and I love it,
Cats are the cutest animal because they're so cuddly.
I like yummy chocolate,
I adore lovely toys when I go to bed,
Dad is as cuddly as a bear.

Katie Grassy (7)
Moyles Court School Limited, Ringwood

Spelling Test

Every Thursday after break is the spelling test,
I'm trembling like an old grandpa who's missed his morning train,
I don't know if I will know next week's spellings,
But I will have a go,
The birds are tweeting loudly,
I think I'm going to faint,
But I must stand my ground.
In the school grounds,
It isn't very easy,
But I must try,
I'm shivering and shaking in my shoes,
And I'm not the best,
In the spelling test.

Isabella Williams (8)
Moyles Court School Limited, Ringwood

Things I Love

My fantastic toys are lovely because they are cute,
I like nice chilli when it is spicy,
Harriet is as grey as the fog,
Swimming is fun because you can splash around,
Singing makes me feel great so I do it all afternoon,
I admire brilliant Miss Christopher.
Dancing makes me feel fantastic so I do dance class on Monday,
I adore beautiful animals because they are cute,
Evie is as beautiful as a rainbow,
I love brownies on Pancake Day,
Puppies are cute when they are playing,
My amazing mum is brilliant when she cooks,
Dylan is adorable while he sleeps.

Zoe Newton (7)
Moyles Court School Limited, Ringwood

Things I Love

I love my fluffy dog because she's cute,
I adore brilliant Egypt while it's hot,
India is brilliant because she's my best friend,
My fantastic dad is brilliant at selling cars,
My terrific mum is beautiful and I love her so much,
I admire brilliant presents at Christmas,
I like yummy chocolate brownies when they're hot,
Singing makes me feel terrific because I love it,
Reading makes me feel elated and I love it,
Evie is as great as a kitten,
India is as lovely as a lily,
Doris is fluffy when she does not go to the groomers,
Easter is fun because it's my favourite time of year.

Poppy Booker (7)
Moyles Court School Limited, Ringwood

Things I Love

I adore my lovely dog because he is so cute,
Snow is as frozen as ice,
I like yummy Pancake Day as I love pancakes,
Flames are as hot as the sun,
I love the terrific owl centre when the show's on,
The zoo is terrific and I love animals,
Acting makes me feel elated because I love it,
Football is brilliant because I play it a lot,
Playing makes me feel wonderful when I'm bored,
Dogs are cute when I tickle their bellies,
My lovely mom is terrific and she is a great cook,
My fluffy cat is excellent when she's jumping.

Evan David Goulding (8)
Moyles Court School Limited, Ringwood

Things I Love

My terrific mummy is brilliant at making food,
I like yummy chocolate when I am allowed it,
I admire terrific toys while having fun,
Cats are brilliant when I give them a hug,
St Lucia is the best because it is hot and fun,
I love lovely clothes because they look good on me,
Dogs are terrific on their backs,
Reading makes me feel brilliant because I like it,
Mummy is as terrific as daffodils and I love her,
My lovely daddy is terrific at playing with me,
Daddy is as wonderful as puppies because he is smooth,
Singing makes me feel terrific but it is hard.

Eloise James (8)
Moyles Court School Limited, Ringwood

Things I Love

Mummy is brilliant when she is with me.
I love my adorable little brother as he is so lovely and cute.
Reading makes me feel elated as I am so good at it.
Chocolate is a yummy food while I am eating it.
Rabbits are brilliant because they are lovely.
Poppy is as great as flowers.
My terrific teacher is brilliant so I give him nice things.
My lovely daddy is terrific when he plays with me,
Acting makes me feel great as I like doing it,
India is as lovely as butterflies,
I adore my lovely rabbit because he is absolutely brilliant.

Jessica Venus (7)
Moyles Court School Limited, Ringwood

Love

Love is bright pink
And tastes of the sweetest strawberries.
It smells of perfumed roses,
And sounds like an orchestra of romantic violins.
Love is a flying arrow, shooting passion into your heart
It is a pristine white dove, flying in the light blue sky.
Love lovingly licks your heart and covers it in emotion,
It is a soothing powder and a creamy lotion.
Love is romantic.

Olivia Walker (9)
Moyles Court School Limited, Ringwood

Excited Is . . .

Excited is helping my mum.
Excited is seeing my cousins.
Excited is having a sleepover at my friend's house.
Excited is going to school.
Excited is having a curry.
Excited is going on holiday.
Excited is seeing my mum and dad.

Tommy Boland (8)
Moyles Court School Limited, Ringwood

Happiness Is . . .

Happiness is hugging my mummy.
Happiness is seeing my pony Ollie.
Happiness is seeing my dad every weekend.
Happiness is giving my dog a hug every morning.
Happiness is when it is sunny.

Ruby Sturton (9)
Moyles Court School Limited, Ringwood

Disgust Strikes Again!

Disgust is a mouldy, dirty green
It tastes like rotten eggs
It will magically spread!
It looks like a huge junk yard, filling walls up high.
It looks as disgusting as sick
Disgust sounds as if someone is about to vomit.
Disgust will make your smile fade away.

Kiera Louise Biles (9)
Portsdown Primary School, Portsmouth

Love For My Sister

She is the blazing ball in my heart. She keeps me going
when I see her.
I am a fire alarm; I scream and screech when I hold her.

When I'm sad, she makes me smile so bright, like a clear
summer's sky!
I will do all in my power to protect her from the lurking evil
That cowardly hides in the shadows.

Supporting her through dark times,
I'm her indestructible shield.
Our love flows like a river; it shall never stop!

I wake up every morning seeing if it's all a dream.
However it is not and I'm happy with that.
No one will stand in-between my love for her.
My love grows each day and it will never stop!

She is the love that fills my heart.
Without her I'm sad, lonely and quiet.
I would be nothing without her, I would only see grey.
I would only feel cold until I see her again.
Then the rainbow should shine brightly again.

She is my one and only: Maddie.
Her name will echo through my life even when my red heart stops.
No love is stronger!

Molly-May Creamer
Portsdown Primary School, Portsmouth

The Wait

Tick, tock, tick, the wait begins.
Will it be the last breath taken?
Or will survival last another day?

My mind is over thinking.
Knots in my stomach twist and turn like struggling snakes,
Whilst my eyes fill with fear for what the future holds.

Constant beads of sweat drip down my tired face,
But I must stay awake,
For it's not time to sleep,
Yet time to wait.

My lips tremble and joy is emptied from my heart.
I look out of a window only to see the traffic
Scurrying like ants across the long roads of spaghetti
Without a care in the world.

I am a shadow amongst the bustle of busy nurses.
I feel weak, but have no stomach for food.
My hands are tense and sickness swallows my trembling,
quivering body.

Yet the clock goes on
Tick . . . tock . . . tick . . . tock
The wait continues.

Blessing Okani (12)
Portsdown Primary School, Portsmouth

Days Of My Life

Rain beads drop furiously
Onto my bowed head.
I sit in a corner,
No one notices me
I am scared.

I'm in a deep, dark forest covered in leaves.
I feel like I want to drown myself,
In the tears of sorrow.
I'm sick to my bones,
Tired of people naming me unwanted.
Throwing me missiles.
Wounding my body and soul.
I am stained
My legs shake in fear
Like a fawn taking its first steps.
My happiness hides behind my soul,
Too scared to appear.
Tied in knots.
My belly is locked together.
I try to keep it in,
But the scream launches out!
I am me but what am I?

Leah Moynihan (10)
Portsdown Primary School, Portsmouth

What Emotion Am I?

My skin is setting on fire,
My ears are steaming wildly,
My face is turning red.
When I can't control myself,
I'm stomping, throwing, screaming,
I can't help myself.
Can you guess what emotion am I?

Sandaru Prabhashwara Kularathne (9)
Portsdown Primary School, Portsmouth

As I Burn Up

Red burning flames swell in my body,
Fury heats my arm, ready to punch him,
A name aimed at me sets off a flaming tornado shooting missiles.
I turn into the Incredible Hulk,
Heat pounds my soul as I push, punch and shove,
Fire shoots from my mouth,
My face is red, my hair's on fire,
What emotion am I?
You don't have time to guess,
I am very impatient,
I am anger!

I'm your reaction,
I'm one of your emotions,
I'm as red as fire,
I'm as hot as the sun,
I'm anger, the furious emotion
Heat pounds my burning heart
As blood fizzles and crackles,
As my red-hot smoke
Turns to flames.

Kyron Brooks (10)
Portsdown Primary School, Portsmouth

Gone But Never Forgotten

Slipping from my eyes,
Streams of sorrow leave tracks of grief and despair.
The hole in my heart is a void
Filled with nothing other than gloom and tragedy.
Memories of him flash through my mind
Like ghostly recalls
As his last bark lingers in the air,
Our last memory races across my mind
And our last walk scars me forever.

Jack Rance (11)
Portsdown Primary School, Portsmouth

What Am I?

Tears run down my face as I sit in the corner.
I can't find my happiness anymore.
It's buried in my soul,
In my deep, deep soul.
Every day and every night getting bullied more and more.
Corners I sit in, yes I do
Names really hurt me and sticks do too.

Walking and walking, I never stop.
I want to drown myself although I cannot.
Night I lay in my bed, not wanting it to be morning again.
My legs are shaking like a metal gate
As I wait for the storm of girls to pass and call me the names.

'Should I tell? No I shouldn't.'
I'm scared, yes I am.
I try to keep it inside yet I have to let it out.
As raindrops fall on me I wonder where I am.
Why? I ask myself.
Why am I so new?
I hope you guess me soon.

Ellie-May Allen (10)
Portsdown Primary School, Portsmouth

Queen Of The United Boredom

Waiting . . . waiting, trying to pass the spare time.
Waiting for the moon to rise. Hoping for the bell to ring.
Wishing for the return of my best friend Joy.

Sometimes I'm hiding, sometimes I'm not
Sometimes I'm . . . does it even matter?

Finally, after days and nights,
I'm filled with excitement as boredom is defeated by Joy.
As usual, slowly the Joy fades away;
Lack of interest comes flooding back again . . . suffocating my world.

Bethany Smith
Portsdown Primary School, Portsmouth

I'm Trying To Help

Her hair falls out, her skin turns grey.
I'd never thought I'd see the one I love fade away.
Tears form in my eyes and crystallise.
What can I do? This can't be true.

Standing in the rain wearing black again
I see her getting carried away, hopefully
She goes to a happy place,
A place where she has lots of space.

After all these years of sitting by her side,
It's so sad that she finally demised.
She let cancer beat her just this once.
I'll make sure I'll visit her every day, every month.

I've become a nurse but it's only gotten worse.
I watch people die every day.
I cry and cry and just hope and pray.
With some people there's just nothing we can do.

But at the end of the day at least
We tried to help all of those who have deceased.

Kezeena Kone
Portsdown Primary School, Portsmouth

Who Am I?

Killer clown's pranks cause me to have pale skin.
Shivering uncontrollably,
Super shaky, sweaty hands tremble.
Eyes flit frantically around the room,
Searching for grave danger.
Hair stands on end,
Prickling my spine with ice-cold fingers.
Please hurry I don't play
The waiting
Game . . .

Levi Kennedy
Portsdown Primary School, Portsmouth

Prison Of Darkness

I'm alone like I'm the last person on Earth,
Dejected, melancholy and disheartened.
Like a grey pavement after the rain
Like a storm cloud waiting to explode with tears
Like an empty bag of sugary delights.

Not saying a word to anyone,
Silent, solemn and lost in my dreams.
Like a forgotten street, which has been dead for an extended period
of time,
Like a dull school with only teachers walking the haunted halls.
Like a ghoul-infested church, when the locals are saying a prayer.

Not telling anyone how I'm feeling,
I'm locked away in my room, away from the dull, grey outside world.
Like a prisoner locked in their cell without anything to eat, drink or
sleep on.
Like an abandoned hospital locked away behind a vast forest,
Like a love for someone that's been locked away inside of them
forever.

Katie Ball
Portsdown Primary School, Portsmouth

Lonely Hour

'An amazing person always crawls into your life.'
That was what my nan said before . . . before she passed away.

Once I knew that, sadness became my closest friend . . .
My only friend. I started to feel alone with sadness
and all I wanted to do was scrunch up into a ball and shed tears.

I'm possessed by someone else and say things I don't mean.
I start to scream into my pillow which starts to sob with me.

I start to feel lost and have flashbacks about my amazing nan.
It's like my heart is a sponge that only absorbs grief.

Leona Ruck
Portsdown Primary School, Portsmouth

As Hot As A Volcano!

Face like a spiky sea urchin
I begin to scream!
Grey fumes block my ears
As I become vermilion.
My blood boils like hot molten lava consuming everything in its way
Without a care in the world.
Temperature rises until it reaches an uncontrollable boiling point.

The red furious flames control me.
I clench my fist as I get annoyed.
The steam train that is in my chest breaks through my ribs.

A hot, fiery tongue shoots out nastiness as I begin to transform.
It feels like I'm changing,
Changing into a monster that hides under your bed at night.
A dragon that prevents my happiness from escaping,
A troll that steals my joy as it tries to cross a bridge.
A vengeful emotion that takes no prisoners.

Fatiah Okubadejo (11)
Portsdown Primary School, Portsmouth

Nerves Have Caught My Tongue!

It all starts. I stand. Told to speak, my hands sweat,
I blush and mutter under my breath, hoping it will all be over soon.
In embarrassment, feeling like dying on the spot,
I wish that the whole world would turn into a speck of dust,
Then miraculously blow away and leave me alone.

It continues. A question, it echoes to the back of the class.
'Taylor!' Going pale, my insides churn and I squeak like a mouse
Under the cruel grasps of hungry, remorseless feline.

It ends. I sit.
Fear sends a cold shiver down my bony,
Vulnerable spine as my peers turn to face the impatient teacher . . .
I breathe out a sigh of relief. It's over!

Tayler Sadler
Portsdown Primary School, Portsmouth

Anger

Stomping, raging, shrieking;
my crimson blood grumbles in my unilluminated veins.
My mind absorbs violent thoughts when I'm called names
or when I'm teased.
I'm completely different person when I lose my temper . . .

I'm a hideous monster: foolish, selfish and thunderous.
I'm a raging bull filled with a scorching blaze.
I feel like I'm the only one.
The only thought I think of is that I'm not normal and I don't belong in
this world.
I'm a completely different person when I lose my temper . . .

The only way to stop is to take an intense breath . . .
I'm no longer a different person . . .
I'm no longer a raging bull . . .
I'm no longer a hideous monster . . .
I'm just an ordinary boy with a delighted feeling.

Peter Russell (11)
Portsdown Primary School, Portsmouth

Sadness

This emotion is in all of us,
Where all the tears and whispers hide,
It comes out with no warning,
It doesn't like to stay inside.

Standing in the darkness,
Crying drops of loneliness,
Not joining in any games,
Being called bad names,

Having bad times,
Causing negative rhymes,
As you see your friends,
Your life bends.

Alfie Lesley James Bignell (11)
Portsdown Primary School, Portsmouth

What Emotion Am I?

My face is red,
Furious and on a rampage,
I smashed a door like a karate student,
Full of stress and feelings of revenge.

I rip the curtains,
With all my might,
Full of fury,
Whilst in a lion fight.

Now I'm wild,
I have lots of ideas,
To really wreck the house,
With fists like Incredible Hulk.

People don't like me,
I don't know why,
Now can you guess who I am?

Nithin Rakesh (8) & Riley
Portsdown Primary School, Portsmouth

Happy Hour

A bright feeling creeps in my mind.
I've missed it tickling my brain like a giggling goblin.
Escaping my mind would mean the world would be a better place.
Although, he must never leave my side,
I will not allow it! I will be nothing without him.
It would be dark.
He makes me happy when I am done for he keeps me company.
However, I wish everyone else could be like me.
A wonderful sunny day, when it's finally Friday (the great half-term holiday).
When I see my best friend Joy.
I embrace the emotion as I would my beloved mother.
Welcome Joy, enter my heart any time!

Archie Griffin (11)
Portsdown Primary School, Portsmouth

I Love To Hate And Hate To Love

It all starts at home; I want to be alone.
Shouting, deafeningly, screaming thunderously
and raging like a rhino.
No one understands me, I'm given many commands.

I hate the words of 'Ollie, Ollie, Ollie, can you play with me?'
This is the moment when the monster inside of me strikes.
I can't control my fury!
I'm a dangerous, devilish dragon demolishing all in my path,
Nothing can get past me.

'Ollie, Ollie, Ollie, can you help me?'
The blood inside of me is like a raging river engulfing my body.

I realise it's time to stop. I breathe out the raging beast inside of me.
The thunderous drum inside me slows its rhythm.
An awkward smile spreads across my face. I roll my eyes.
Almost. 'Ollie, Ollie, Ollie!'

Oliver Atkins
Portsdown Primary School, Portsmouth

Knotted Inside

Grinding teeth, chattering heart,
I wait as the hours pass by.
Cuddling myself, hugging my soul as shadows cross my darkened
room.
Windows with eyes above, images inside,
Arms outstretched, bony fingers claw
And bloodied hands scurry up my wall
Not leaving my bed, I falter with fear,
Black clouds fill my thoughts, red mist shrouds my eyes.
Sitting in my corner with stomach twisted,
Tying me in knots every day.
I weep with futility, helpless with my thoughts
And I cry and cry and cry.

Carlie Traviss
Portsdown Primary School, Portsmouth

Days Go By

School goes by like
I'm living in a nightmare.
Days go by like a snail,
Thinking of you again every minute of every day.
I hide away, wishing you were here.
By my side again.
Tears stream down my cheeks,
Slowly and painfully scaring my face.
Thoughts of you ache in my heart.
Flash past my brain and burrow in my soul.
Remembering every time we've spent together.
Is painful, trying not to forget your look,
Your touch or your voice.
Just one more hug, just one more chance.
To say goodbye, is that to much to ask?
What emotion am I?

Taia Hewett (10)
Portsdown Primary School, Portsmouth

The Anger Of My Brain!

The anger of my brain haunts me every day!
I walk glumly into school; my peers stare and glare at me like I'm
crazy.

The only colour I see in my head is vermilion
The colour of the horned, crimson count
who hunts my joy and ruthlessly destroys it.

Hell lives in the deepest places in my soul and when it bursts out,
like the roaring of a dinosaur trying to assert its dominance,
it spreads a sea of rage across my body.

The only emotion I see is anger! I'll shout! I'll scream!
Anger is the most vicious, soul-eating emotion around.

Harry Lowden
Portsdown Primary School, Portsmouth

What's Wrong With You?

Are you happy, snappy or feeling a bit sassy?
What's wrong?
Please don't cry you're not up so high!

You're in the corner with nothing to do
You're feeling sad, what's wrong with you?

Drowning in tears,
You have nothing to fear,
Everybody loves you
You just can't see who
Poor you.

You're lost in your mind
While feeling behind
Is somebody talking about you,
Just because you are new?

Kiera Louise Biles (9) & Vimbai
Portsdown Primary School, Portsmouth

The Brave Fight

I remember when you said we'll be friends forever
but I don't see you around now.
I miss the day when we first went to school
and you held my hand the whole way, reassuring me of your
presence.

Nothing can come between us as we are bound by courage.
You've been there through my thick and thins,
my ups and downs and my darkest times.

When mean girls fought you gave me the courage to fight back.
The day I walked home alone it was dark,
you gave me the power to carry on.

I returned the favour and gave you all my courage
whilst you battled cancer and broke free from its curse.

Georgia Smith
Portsdown Primary School, Portsmouth

Sadness

Sadness is grey; it tastes like a sour sweet in my mouth,
It smells so disgusting that I feel sick.
It feels like a fragile bomb has been forcefully shoved
down my throat.
I feel so sad that I start to cry. It reminds me of all the times
I have felt sad.

Help me! I am drowning in my own tears,
Betrayed by my own emotions, waiting for somebody
to come save me.
Save me!

I fight and I fight but nothing happens!
My stomach twists and turns as my heart burns.
How can this turn, turn around? I can't breathe, I am in agony!
I am fading away! Help me!

Kiana Robinson (10)
Portsdown Primary School, Portsmouth

Too Shy To Rhyme

As shy as a ghost, I hide away nervously from the confident souls
that drag my conviction down into the darkest depths of
my inner being.
I lie low, shy immersed in the shadows whilst everyone
else dances joyfully,
ignoring me like I am invisible, like I don't exist.
Suddenly I am noticed. A strange and uncomfortable feeling
shivers up my spine;
I am asked to stand and talk at the front of the class,
the room of doom.
Eyes burn into my heart, melting away my ability to speak.
My mind whispers for me to run away but my legs betray me
and do not move.
I am frozen in my shyness.

Emily Wood
Portsdown Primary School, Portsmouth

Beast

Slamming the door and shouting at the head teacher
I can't believe what I did!
What am I?
Getting my fists ready to punch
And smashing the window with a hammer.
What am I?

Clenching my shoulders, tightly hunched
And cannon-balling through the door
No one can touch me.
What am I?

Flames flow through my body, heart pulsing in my face.
I am red, I am black, I am scary.
What am I?

Tommy Fred Thomas-Smith-Carter (10)
Portsdown Primary School, Portsmouth

Raging Bull

Red
Explosions
Fill my head
With crazy zigzags
Like lightning bolts in
Multicoloured patterns.
Boiling, bubbling, seething.
My fist is ready to punch a window, a door, anything.
Hot lava is leaving a trail of fury behind me,
A burning deep and leaving scars.
Bubbling Resentment and Sulking are my names.
What am I?

Carmen Elizabith Richards (10)
Portsdown Primary School, Portsmouth

Anger Like Never Before

Red rage lurking in the air and I'm ready to pounce on my victim.
Fury like thunder in a raging storm and my fists bunch into rocks.
Terrifying tantrums and my behaviour out of control.
Name-calling gets me past the point to where I'm like a bull ready to
charge.
Deafening screams like repeating rockets racing through my veins
With firework sparks exploding in my head.
Temper, like fire, spilling out of my mouth,
Molten lava shooting acid words out of a vast crater
And spitting into the air, poisoning and toxic.
Displeasure fills the ears of everyone around me,
The looks on their faces . . . Petrified!

Frankie Pullen (11)
Portsdown Primary School, Portsmouth

Broken . . .

Eyes tragically morph into a cascading waterfall,
plummeting like liquid bombs of sorrow.
Crying like the low spirited wind.
Remorseful, terrifying tears suffocate my joy,
washing away any remaining fragment of laughter.

The pain of depression rules my world, rules my core, rules my soul.

My soul, lifeless and dull, drowns into the sinking sea of grim misery.
My heart like a sponge, sucks up all the sadness
as flashbacks of distress strike me like lightning,
dragging me from the light and into the cruel grasp of unforgiving
darkness.

Leah Cooper
Portsdown Primary School, Portsmouth

The Redness Of Anger

I feel like a vicious, violent volcano about to erupt on innocent lives!
I feel like I'm full of molten lava, a bubbling beast building inside of me, ready to burst!

I look as red as dynamite about to explode on innocent children!
I feel like a snake slowly suffocating the atmosphere around me!

I try to control it but it has already taken over my mind!
Lightning strikes my brain, making it turn against me.

The Devil ruthlessly sticks its venomous fangs into my brain!
The storm crashes its atomic waves onto my heavy heart!

I am the redness of Anger!

Bradley Moger
Portsdown Primary School, Portsmouth

Fear Strikes

Fear is here, ready to introduce nightmares into the panic room of slumber.
I'm waiting for the moon's job to be done
and the golden blazing knight to save me, picturing . . . picturing.
I picture a demon from Hell. A silhouette? A mirage? The real thing?

My cover acts as an invisible cloak;
a naive tactic of camouflage yet I still do it every time.
The night always feels longer than the day.
Every creak of the floor, every scratch in the distance
is fear crawling sensitively towards me.
Each night I survive. I wonder when it will be my time?

Chesney Poulton (10)
Portsdown Primary School, Portsmouth

Riddle Of Emotions

Knots in my stomach
Feeling high,
Up in the sky,
Legs shaking like a metal gate,
This isn't great
What emotion am I?
I'll give you some clues
So you won't lose
But remember I don't like to wait.

Maria Danan (8), Maileigh & Marvel
Portsdown Primary School, Portsmouth

The Siblings Are Coming!

It all starts at home; I want to play alone.
I want to have peace and quiet but my little brothers and sisters run like a herd of raging rhinos with uncontrollable energy.
I hate it when they say, 'Bradley! Can you chase us?'
I turn into a beast looking for prey; I am not to be messed with!
I dangerously destroy everything in sight. I feel like I need to stop.
I breathe out the raging monster
and the emotion of anger leaves me for another day.

Bradley Shaun Thomas-Smith-Carter (10)
Portsdown Primary School, Portsmouth

Anger

I live in the darkest, dullest places of the world.
My ears steam forever
Anger adapts to the dark, dull Underworld.
Please, Anger get off me.
I don't want you in my brain.
Anger shouts at everybody like my daddy.
Please, please Anger, get off me,
I don't want you with me anymore.

Oscar Brossier (9)
Portsdown Primary School, Portsmouth

Fear Rises!

Screaming . . . screaming as loud as a roar!
If I shout, you will know.
If I do I will make you bored.
Waiting . . . waiting in peace, I watched the darkness arise.
Looking at the creepy, dark shadows whilst keeping myself safe.
When I shout, I will give you a scare.
If I do that I will eat you to pieces.

Connor Swinndells (11)
Portsdown Primary School, Portsmouth

What Emotion Am I?

I sit in the corner
Clenching my fists together,
A face full of desperate fury.
I face fear each and every week.
I see things run across my room
Leaving tracks to the cupboard.

Bradley Hayward (10)
Portsdown Primary School, Portsmouth

Battling Dragons

Battling dragons,
Slicing blood-covered flesh,
Glistening, tinted silver,
Tumbling over rigid ground,
Continuing battling.
What emotion am I?

Zak Blandford (9) & Callum
Portsdown Primary School, Portsmouth

Anger Has Escaped

A nger is forever in the dimension of Hell,
N ever come here,
G iant volcanoes on every island,
E veryone viciously stomping everywhere,
R evenge is here.

Preston Maclean (9) & Frazer
Portsdown Primary School, Portsmouth

Anger Feels Your Body

A nger races through your body, showing in your faces.
N ever stop stomping and making loads of sound
G oing crazy instead of being lazy
E very word is shouted out loud
R eally loud and crazy.

Mark Hanna (8)
Portsdown Primary School, Portsmouth

Anger Strikes Back!

A nger lives in the Underworld, trapped
N ow he has escaped
G aining power to make me mad!
E vil loves him, he is its king.
R unning away from the Emotion Guards shouting, 'Help!'

Elliot Stafford (9)
Portsdown Primary School, Portsmouth

Happy

I'm happy, I'm happy outside in the sun playing up above me.
The birds sing up high in the sky and flying and flying, they were in the nest.
Late at night they're fast asleep. *Zzzz*
They wake up in the morning and they fall down to the grass.

Mareace Buffong (8)
St Augustine Of Canterbury RC Primary School, Gillingham

Grace's Happiness!

Happiness is the sound of Noah's laughter rippling through
our house.
Happiness is the sound of the school bell ringing at 3:30pm
on Friday,
The weekend has begun!
Happiness is the taste of my yummy cakes as they come
out of the oven.
Happiness is the feel of my soft cushion resting against my face.
Happiness is having an evening snuggle on the sofa with my family.
Happiness is people having fun around the world and laughing.
Happiness is seeing the first flash of lights on the Christmas tree.
Happiness is the smell of candyfloss cooking in the machine.
Happiness is the smell of my delicious cakes cooking in the oven.

Grace Prestidge (9)
St Augustine Of Canterbury RC Primary School, Gillingham

My Grandad

My grandad is a lovely man,
Any time I need him,
He'll do all he can.
He's very strong and always good
Whenever I cuddle him,
He smells like cedar wood.
Whenever I see him,
I never feel bad
Especially when he plays angry crab!
If grandads had to do a test,
My grandad would win
Because he is the best.

Jack Marvell (8)
St Augustine Of Canterbury RC Primary School, Gillingham

Love For A Girl Like Me!

I was a girl with a normal life
My world happily expanded when you made me your wife,
I love you deeply and everyone can see
You mean more than any treasure to me.
Any time I needed a cuddle you were there.
And I for you, of course that's how we care
Our love can shine and is truly the best
We'll live our lives together in happiness.

Keira Hope (9)
St Augustine Of Canterbury RC Primary School, Gillingham

Joy!

Never doubting
Always sprouting
with Joy!

Always happy
Never snappy
Because it's a gift of happiness and peace.

Come and join the fun
It's an easy sum
Because it's there, I promise you; somewhere deep
down in your heart.

It's never not there because if you unburied the lost you will find.
It somewhere waiting to be spotted,
Excited to pass from person to person,
To spread until the world is nothing but Joy!

Nothing but Joy is the word of love and love takes a whole
bundle of it.

Daisy Marianne Gray (9)
St Augustine Of Canterbury RC Primary School, Gillingham

Delightful Butlins!

D azzling people stare around
E veryone has massive smiles
L ovely rides make a sound
I see queues stretch for miles
G o and find your favourite funfair
H earing music makes my heart beat
T ruly excited voices fill the air
F lying swings, I clutch onto my seat
U p, up, Red Arrows fly in the blue sky
L ooping and swooping round and round

B ravo, bravo as the Red Arrows scream goodbye
U nder umbrellas joyful faces follow the sound,
T remendous crowds wait for the show to begin
L ights glisten in my eyes,
I love it as Diversity run in
N ever-ending crowds yell excited cries
S adly it is time to say goodbye.

Maria Vesey (9)
St Augustine Of Canterbury RC Primary School, Gillingham

Antarctic Anger

As bad as the weather, as bad as the sea
Anger keeps burning up interestingly
Even though dislike is wanting good luck
It always finds a way of tripping him up.
As a matter of fact as he can see
His anger is having a jubilee!
He sees there's a way of a frown.
It can also mean anger makes him feel a bit down.
If he wants something merry, if he wants something happy
He should go to the kitchen and get some honey!
Now he sees he doesn't want to be angry.
He just wants to be a lot more cheery!

Methembe Mathinta (8)
St Augustine Of Canterbury RC Primary School, Gillingham

Joy!

Joy is a happy time for me and for you,
Thinking of lots of things to do,
When we think of happy times,
These go buzzing through our minds.

When a new baby smiles,
Or a child runs for miles,
When birthday bells ring,
All the children sing.

When you get a pet,
There's no need to fret,
You'll be as happy as can be,
Just you wait and see.

Seeing your parents,
Or spending time with your grandparents,
Brings a smile to your face,
Which is when joy comes into place.

Paige Allen (8)
St Augustine Of Canterbury RC Primary School, Gillingham

Out And About In The Snow . . .

H earing snow
E veryone stomping about
A aron, Jack and Cole are out
R ide your bike
I n a hike
N oses so cold you can't smell anything
G ot to build a snowman

S ummertime coming
N o more snowman
O ranges grow now
W intertime is behind.

Harry Louis Lamarque (10)
St Augustine Of Canterbury RC Primary School, Gillingham

Madness

Sometimes I'm happy, sometimes I'm sad,
Sometimes things happen that make me turn mad!
Like my sister rummaging amongst my things,
Hiding my toys and taking my rings.
My stomach, it churns, my heart, it goes thump,
I really feel now I am getting the hump!
She's been in my room, I can tell straight away,
There's a certain amount of confused disarray.
My pulse, it is racing, my face has turned red,
The pressure is building inside of my head,
Now this is the part that everyone dreads,
I let out a scream from the top of my head,
The windowpanes shake,
The glass starts to shatter and Mummy shouts out,
'Rosie, what is the matter?'
Exhausted I cry, but Mum holds me tight,
I retire to my bed for the rest of the night.

Rosie Ellis (8)
St Augustine Of Canterbury RC Primary School, Gillingham

My Happy Life

What makes me really happy is spending time with Mum and Paul.
I also love my Xbox, my Lego game does rule.

Tomorrow I go to the school church and this makes me very glad,
Then sometimes after school I like to go visit my dad.

Sometimes I'm as bright and happy as a star to be with my loving family.
We have a few laughs and have a great time and they are always there for me.

If you like this poem I'll be as shocked as electricity,
But if you don't mind because I'm happy being me.

Liam Taylor (8)
St Augustine Of Canterbury RC Primary School, Gillingham

Never Been Happier

So why can this be?
Super sunny skies is all I can see,
I'm in a wonderful place with all my friends and family.
We all tuck into a super yummy feast with grapes galore and
chocolate cake.
Mmm my favourite treat.
Beautiful colourful flowers are all around us.
Me and my friends play under the warm sunny breeze.
Home we go now, our fantastic day has come to an end,
And I say goodbye to all my friends. Am I sad?
No, no way! I've had the most wonderful day.
Now I'm back in Heaven, so why can this be?
Because I am snuggled in bed with my super favourite teddy.
I have never been happier.

Isabella Maria Susan Barritt (8)
St Augustine Of Canterbury RC Primary School, Gillingham

Loving School

When the bell rings school starts,
People dashing, dancing towards class,
Teacher telling children what to do,
Playtime, let's play football.

Loving lunch every day,
Now it's time to go and play,
Whistle, whistle, lunch is over,
Back to class we go.

Clay making, poster making,
Getting messy, drawing pictures.
Time to get ready to go
Ring, ring, time to go,
Everyone thinking, *best school day ever!*

Hayden Gray (9)
St Augustine Of Canterbury RC Primary School, Gillingham

105

Leave Me Alone

Walking along, looking over my shoulder,
Hoping and hoping it will soon be over.
Every day I'm worried to death,
That they will catch me up, so I hold my breath.

Each step I take is a torment as I make my way home,
Praying and praying that they leave me alone.
Why do they do it? Does it make them feel proud?
Does beating me up, make them stand out from the crowd?

They kick and they punch me, letting out their anger,
Do they like hurting me? I sometimes wonder.
I am almost home, the nightmare is over,
So there'll be no more looking over my shoulder.

Tifainè Tomlinson (11)
St Augustine Of Canterbury RC Primary School, Gillingham

Be Forgiving

Someone has upset me
And hurt me so I cried,
Even though I'm hurting,
I still see their good side.

I don't want to lose our friendship,
But I need to know you care,
Because I can't imagine what
It would be like if you were not there.

So we should all remember
Instead of caring less,
We would be much happier,
If we use . . . forgiveness!

Holly Burton (7)
St Augustine Of Canterbury RC Primary School, Gillingham

I'm Feeling Angry!

I'm feeling angry, I'm feeling mad,
I think I'll be naughty, I think I'll be bad.
Mum made me come off my PlayStation 4,
She says too much screen time makes me a bore.
'Off now,' she says, 'come off and play, it's a warm and sunny day.
Fresh air and exercise is good for you, it's what all young boys
should do.'
I feel more angry and I start to frown as Mum puts her head down.
She stares at her iPad screen for a couple of hours, which I
think is mean.
But my mood gets better after tea, it's back on my PlayStation
for me.

Oliver Patrick Byrne (10)
St Augustine Of Canterbury RC Primary School, Gillingham

Feelings Of Emotions!

Joy is sun yellow.
It reminds me of a baby's smile.
Sadness is plain grey.
It feels like a raindrop had just landed on my head.
Anger is raging red.
It feels like a bomb exploded.
Fear is ghost white.
It sounds like deafening screams from a haunted house!
Disgust is lime green.
It reminds me of looking out the window and seeing a stormy day.

Evie Thompson (9)
St Augustine Of Canterbury RC Primary School, Gillingham

Happy Holiday

H appy holiday, I'm so excited
O n my way to the sparkling, sunny sun
L ong flight on an aeroplane, looking forward to the films
I n the swimming pool, laughing and joking, having fun in the sun.
D onald, Mickey and others to meet us for breakfast, can't wait, feeling happy.
A t last we are off to the park for a day, roller coaster as tall as Mount Everest
Y awning on the drive home, tired after a great holiday in the sunny sun.

Joseph Robert Dunn (8)
St Augustine Of Canterbury RC Primary School, Gillingham

The Unhelpful Anger!

Anger, anger, anger he's always on a hanger.
Anger, anger, anger he has a rude manager.
Anger, anger, anger walks into the shop asking for another super angry sweet.

Anger, anger, anger gets the anger from Donald Duck.
Anger, anger, anger is at home watching another episode of Mickey Mouse.

Anger has a weird life.
Anyway Anger never ever gives up on anything.

Hope Asuen'mhen (10)
St Augustine Of Canterbury RC Primary School, Gillingham

Happiness

H ope and joy, love and peace
A warm cuddle from my family
P arties in light with laughter and giggles,
P eace for God and faith in him
I n peace is love for us to share,
N ice friends sharing kindness
E veryone is a friend to each other
S adness is to be made happiness
S o many kind things to be grateful for.

Samantha Shaw (8)
St Augustine Of Canterbury RC Primary School, Gillingham

Christmas Joy

C hristmas
H olly wreath on the door
R eindeer pulling Santa's sleigh
I ce-cold outside
S anta is coming to town
T insel on the tree
M ass in the church
A men
S tockings.

Jake Morgan (8)
St Augustine Of Canterbury RC Primary School, Gillingham

Laughter

L aughter is created by people around you, when you make them
smile
A ll of your friends make you chuckle at some time or another
U nusual things make me giggle!
G iggles give you hiccups and butterflies in your belly
H appiness surrounds me
T erry, our car, takes us out for a fun drive
E veryone is my friend
R ound the world laughter spreads to you and me.

Grace Goldup (9)
St Augustine Of Canterbury RC Primary School, Gillingham

Love . . .

True love comes from the heart,
Not from the head,
Love never fades,
It flows on and on continuously.

People who think about love in their head
Are most likely to never know true love,
So remember
Love is in the inside and not on the outside.

Ashleyne Reen (9)
St Augustine Of Canterbury RC Primary School, Gillingham

You Are Hungry, What Do You Do?

Y ou can eat from whatever plate you want!
O ver the top sometimes we go
U SA, Italy, France, there are so many places you can eat

E at, go on it's the time
A nd it's dinner so you eat
T ime to eat!

Marco Capolupo (10)
St Augustine Of Canterbury RC Primary School, Gillingham

Emotions

E xpressions of feelings deep in my soul,
M oods changing depending on circumstances.
O vercome by different sensations; fear replaced by
T enderness, when I see those I love.
I nstinctive and intuitive senses
O pening up my mind and changing my world – there's
N ever a dull moment!
S cience struggles to define emotions.

Conor Whittaker (10)
St Augustine Of Canterbury RC Primary School, Gillingham

This Is Anger

Inside my tummy a volcano sits,
I look in my mirror, my face is steaming red.
I try to be happy but I can't.
Suddenly a fire starts burning in my bones,
I keep trying to be happy but I can't.
I clench my fist, my cheeks are red,
I start to rage.
This is anger.

Jake Harlow (9)
St Augustine Of Canterbury RC Primary School, Gillingham

Kindness

K indness is something that's very cheap.
I t can easily be shown in how we speak.
N ever treat anyone in a nasty way
D ecide to be kind to everyone every day
N ever be naughty or hurt anyone
E veryone can have fun
S pecial gifts from up above
S hould be shown as God's daily love.

Amelia Hope (8)
St Augustine Of Canterbury RC Primary School, Gillingham

Fear

A fright of flying fear flying through the darkest night.
A hand, a scream, the cold black fear is here . . .
I run and hide but it's no use, it's here!
Holding on so very tight, I'm afraid and all alone.
I see a light, a shining light coming closer and closer.

Blake Parker (10)
St Augustine Of Canterbury RC Primary School, Gillingham

Flowers And Butterflies

It is a beautiful summer's day.
The sun is shining, flowers are popping up everywhere.
Butterflies are landing on my brown silky hair, tied up in a long
ponytail.
One landed on my finger, and a tiny little tickle for a sneeze,
My dog Brownie was happy playing with my friend's dog.
I was happy standing next to my friend Kate smiling.

Annabelle Laffar (9)
St Cuthbert Mayne Catholic Primary School, Cranleigh

The Dog Watches

As the dog watches the man falls
The thump of a body, a howl of Hell.
Flanders is where the dog played,
He ran, he leapt, he was at his best,
But when there was war there was no turning back,
No turning back to normality.

His owner screamed, he said to 'run'
But the dog stood there stunned.
But finally he did what his owner said
So he ran back to the trenches lonely, heartbroken.

He didn't know why but he was like a father to him,
They played, they jumped, they even sang!
He looked after him and treated him with respect.
But there was one thing he remembered,
One thing that was important.

A dog only lives twice,
When sometimes saves you from the pound
And when someone saves you from a bullet.
He was the man who saved his life.
He was the one who cared.

Feargus Whalley (8)
St Cuthbert Mayne Catholic Primary School, Cranleigh

Scared

I feel scared when I watch a horror movie,
And when I am in the dark
I have so many nightmares, actually too many to count.
About clowns, ogres, dragons, giants, death, monsters
But the scariest of all are about the horror games.
Don't go browsing horror games because you'll really get a shock

So search good things on the Internet
Or you will see what my nightmares are like.

Ruby Templeman (9)
St Cuthbert Mayne Catholic Primary School, Cranleigh

Guilty

I am so guilty,
I have just eaten some chocolate cake,
I hope no one will notice,
my mum and dad will be so mad,
I will go up to my room for one hour.

I am so guilty,
I know what I have done,
I want to shout and scream on my back
for I know what is wrong.

Early today I woke up,
I heard arguments as horrible as a storm,
I edged closer and realised it was about the chocolate cake I ate last
night,
I think they were arguing about who ate the chocolate cake.
I think I should go and tell them,
shouldn't I?
I just told them,
and they were pleased with me.

Amber Carter (8)
St Cuthbert Mayne Catholic Primary School, Cranleigh

What Makes Me Calm

Calm is the greatest feeling
Going for walks in the countryside makes me calm.
Cuddling my teddy makes me calm.
Watching the rain makes me calm.

I'm as calm as the breeze rushing past in the sky.
You can be calm in different ways.
You can be calm if everything's quiet.
Wait, listen, that's not always true,
Birds whistling while wind is blowing can be calm.

Georgia Inwood (9)
St Cuthbert Mayne Catholic Primary School, Cranleigh

115

The Sandman

He opens up your energy tank until it's empty,
During one day though,
He'll fill it up but only in your bed!
His sand is as yellow as earwax,
But only this falls in your eyes.

He will make you want to yawn,
Until the light of dawn,
As soon as your head hits the pillow,
You'll be in the land of nod.
His sand is a bullet of sleep,
Hits you in the eye.

He'll make you feel tired,
And count sheep,
As many as a million
But whatever happens
The Sandman is on his way.

Jozef Edward Bokota (9)
St Cuthbert Mayne Catholic Primary School, Cranleigh

When I'm Terrified

When I'm scared I scream and hide,
Eyes like saucers, nervously shaking,
Curled up in a ball, bursting into tears,
'Go away Monster, please don't nip my ears!'

My mouth tastes bitter,
My tongue like a desert,
The monster is going to get me,
I know it too.

Now I understand,
Why people get terrified,
I didn't know the horrible feeling before,
But now I do.

Molly Gardiner (8)
St Cuthbert Mayne Catholic Primary School, Cranleigh

Anger Is Bad

Anger is a weird feeling,
It comes out of your body when you least expect it,
He lives in the deepest places.
He is as big as a volcano and as bad as lava,
Everyone is scared of him,
If he takes one step out they all run away.
Once he comes out he never goes away.
He'll scream and he'll shout,
Everyone will hide till he is not around.

His face is all red and his skin is rough and spiky,
If he comes out try and run away,
Try and stay calm and stay out of sight.
Anger is bad and might even bite,
A good thing to do is to stay out of sight,
Anger is bad when it is out of control,
It will keep on going until you stop it.

Riya Viradia (9)
St Cuthbert Mayne Catholic Primary School, Cranleigh

Anger

It will give pain to another emotions,
It will make him glad
He likes to be mean to Happy and Sad
No one can calm his temper
In fun and games,
He likes to trash them
No one likes him
He is the toughest around
He is spawned by the devils in the graves
It makes him angry, saying that he'll rip and tear
He can be anywhere
So you better watch out
He'll kick and scream until he fades like smoke.

Luca Alessio James Lo Russo (8)
St Cuthbert Mayne Catholic Primary School, Cranleigh

Happiness

It was a rainy day, but she was still happy.
She was even happier than a dog with a bone,
Even happier than a cat with some fish,
Even happier than a bird with a worm,
Even happier than a horse with an apple,
She was even happier than a squirrel with a nut.
The enormous smile on her face
Could brighten up one thousand sailors in a storm.
The rain was roaring down terribly with rage,
But no bubbling anger filled her heart.
She became even happier when the rain stopped . . .
Puddles to jump in!

Kallia Pantelis (9)
St Cuthbert Mayne Catholic Primary School, Cranleigh

Miserable

Being miserable is the worst

It climbs inside and slits you,
But all it really is like a creepy ghost
And he groans and moans and no one can hear anything!

But if only Happy was here he'd brighten up everything.
Miserable is sad and lies underground
And is the second most feared around!

He's green, slimy, cold and wet
And can be annoying but it's only a spiky emotion and crawls
underground.

Julian King (9)
St Cuthbert Mayne Catholic Primary School, Cranleigh

Happy

Happy is my best thing to be.
Happy is everyone's best thing, it can make people laugh.
Happy is as good as the sun.
Sometimes happy can end.
Happy is great, happy can be lots of different things.
Happy is as good as a lollipop
Happy is awesome
Happy is what people love
Happy is always in us.

Fraser James Philp (9)
St Cuthbert Mayne Catholic Primary School, Cranleigh

Happy

I jumped and jumped until I was in space,
I fell back down.
I went sideways and went to London
And went back to space and fell back down.
I jumped and I jumped till I went to Africa.
Till I went back to London and then back to space.
This adventure was great.
And happy is better than five monkeys laughing their heads off.
I laughed and laughed all the way until I landed.

Jessica Jones (9)
St Cuthbert Mayne Catholic Primary School, Cranleigh

Untitled

Anger is like a hot ball of fire, it's the fiercest emotion around,
And you can't hold him in until he's back underground.
Boiling like a volcano he won't go away until you learn to
hold him inside.
Anger lives down in a deep slimy bog
And won't go away until he wants to calm down.
Things like kicking make Anger appear
And we'll all run away until he stops and goes back.
Cuddles and happiness block Anger out until he can't hold it back.

Emma Moran (8)
St Cuthbert Mayne Catholic Primary School, Cranleigh

Excited

Excited is a good feeling
It takes you away to a land of excitement, where you feel happy.
Excited is a good feeling.
Excited makes me feel as happy as a dog with a bone.
Sometimes it makes you cry as you feel so happy.
I love the feeling excited.
It makes me hyper sometimes.
But when the feeling goes I don't feel as good.

Kornelia Kin (9)
St Cuthbert Mayne Catholic Primary School, Cranleigh

Confused

Confused is a weird feeling.
It jumps out when you least expect it
It lives up above in that mushy part of your brain.
Confused takes you prisoner in a cage of clouds
Like you're in some sort of confused land.
Time feels like it's frozen and Confused swoops over you.
The only way to get rid of it is by listening and learning.
So listen and learn and Confused can't get to you.

Cathal Jabbur (9)
St Cuthbert Mayne Catholic Primary School, Cranleigh

I Always Feel This Emotion

I feel this emotion most of the time.
When I'm out and about and all over town.
Every holiday I go on a smile pops on my face.
Happy is the best, everyone likes him.
Happy is a speeding bullet.
He only comes out when you're not feeling sad.
He always comes out to make you feel glad.

Mia Kennett (8)
St Cuthbert Mayne Catholic Primary School, Cranleigh

Excited

Excitement comes out when you are happy,
You jump for joy like a kangaroo.
It's an amazing feeling to have,
You feel so good,
You can't wait for what is happening
So you squeal and squirm, twist and turn.

Sophia Craig (8)
St Cuthbert Mayne Catholic Primary School, Cranleigh

Anger

Anger is not a nice feeling.
You go out of control.
You shout and scream until you calm down.
You lose your temper so much you tend to hit them.
Anger makes people sad.
You sometimes make people sad, then you get told off.

Alfie Mark George Nye (8)
St Cuthbert Mayne Catholic Primary School, Cranleigh

Love

I love my family.
I love them more than gold.
Nothing can stop me from loving my family.
I love my family as much as the shooting stars
They love me and I love them.

Margot Sophie Harmsworth (9)
St Cuthbert Mayne Catholic Primary School, Cranleigh

Excited

Excited is a happy feeling although it can be bad,
Sometimes you can have butterflies,
Sometimes you don't have anything,
You get those feelings when you move somewhere new,
Excited is a happy feeling, it makes you like a frolicking lamb.

Leini Kay-Russell (9)
St Cuthbert Mayne Catholic Primary School, Cranleigh

Scared

Scared is a weird feeling,
You get shaky legs as wobbly as jelly,
It is something that happens naturally, there's nothing you can do,
Love will heal the scared feeling inside,
So be brave and stop that not nice feeling.

Abigail Southwell (8)
St Cuthbert Mayne Catholic Primary School, Cranleigh

Fear

Fear is bad, you should never be afraid.
When you are afraid your knees start to shake!
You get a lump in your throat
You feel so sick
But then you feel brave.

Dylan Shorter (8)
St Cuthbert Mayne Catholic Primary School, Cranleigh

Joy

Bubbly,
Fun, sunny,
Energetic as a puppy
Delighted, joyful
Excited
A key to a new world,
Cheerful, merry,
Joy.

Evangeline Bailey (8)
St Lawrence CE Primary School, Sevenoaks

Anger

Rage,
Short-fused, infuriated
Screwed up to be angry at anyone,
So furious you would break anyone's soul,
So furious you would break everything,
Fired up, annoyed
Raged
Anger!

Fergus Mylroi (7)
St Lawrence CE Primary School, Sevenoaks

Thunder And Joy

Be a man with anger management,
You are insane, unbalanced and sick,
You have got rage coming out your ears,
Like red-hot fury.
Your friend is off the rails
You are insane.

Stop being mad and insane,
Be joyful now,
You have got a golden heart,
With roses and happiness,
Sprinkled on top.
Be careful and elegant,
Like whoever you want,
Just imagine.

Jemma Robson (10)
St Lawrence CE Primary School, Sevenoaks

Anger

A livid flame,
Spreads through your body,
Raging theories,
Stay alive.

Throughout the world,
Bitter lives,
Live once more.

Today is the day,
Get payback
For what's yours.

Aimee Elisabeth Lloyd (10)
St Lawrence CE Primary School, Sevenoaks

Anger

Livid, flaming, red-hot fury,
As angry as a charging bull,
A burst of rage,
A mad, bitter rage never to be controlled,
Fierce,
Strong,
Daring,
Agitated,
Stressed,
Tearing out his hair,
The boss has arrived,

Revengeful,
Ready for battle,
Hell's at his back.

Ellie Reeve (11)
St Lawrence CE Primary School, Sevenoaks

Fear

A storm of fear inside his body,
Appalled by his craziness,
Troubled, nervous, unbalanced,
Concerned he'll be hunted down.

Terrified, white-lipped, afraid,
Disturbed through fright
Distressed with regret,
Fearfulness, fearful, feared,

Hot under the collar,
Bad news was coming his way and he knew it!

Stephanie Mack (10)
St Lawrence CE Primary School, Sevenoaks

The Sandman

Hopeless, miserable old man,
Cheerless along a long, winding road,
A sad let-down man on a lonely road,
A dull man along the road, out of sight of all people,
A painful man on the road,

A dull, sad man on a dusty road,
Walking on the footpath where no one sees him,
Dashing hopes of a great life ahead,
No one sees him, not even the one or two people walking past him.
Wanting a great life but he gets nothing, not even a great life.

William Charles Bourner Prescott (10)
St Lawrence CE Primary School, Sevenoaks

Broken-Hearted

Blue, downhearted,
A dark shadow,
Full of gloom and sorrow
Heart of dust,
Destroyed friendship,
Forlorn, lonely,
A shivery feeling made his whole body tremble with fear,
Alone, frightened,
A deserted island,
Sadness tore him apart.

Amy Fairservice (10)
St Lawrence CE Primary School, Sevenoaks

The Boss!

Raging, livid,
Battle ready,
The boss!

Fierce, bitter,
Balling up with rage,
Someone's out of line!

Outraged, annoyed,
He's going to erupt like a volcano,
You better stand back!

Rebecca Padley (10)
St Lawrence CE Primary School, Sevenoaks

Shocked

Startled, surprised, upset
The thought of it trickled down his spine
Heart scared
Overwhelmed with fear
Stress struck him.

He was deserted
Whole life turned upside down
His heart was broken and blue
He was turned down!

Olivia Petersen (9)
St Lawrence CE Primary School, Sevenoaks

On The Battlefield

Prepared for battle
I tried to muffle
All the things in my mind but
Nothing stands
On the battlefield.

On the battlefield
The grievousness
Was palpable
In the battle.

Daniel Pengelly (11)
St Lawrence CE Primary School, Sevenoaks

Emotions

Hopeless, cheerful,
Sad, bliss,
Which one will you pick?
Joyful, sorrowful,
Emotions are amazing,
Depressed, bright,
Happy, miserable,
Sometimes horrible,
Sometimes brilliant!

Lachlan Moir (9)
St Lawrence CE Primary School, Sevenoaks

Anger

Anger, hate,
Horrible, annoyed anger lay deep down
With all the mixed and mangled monsters.
Nightmares punished Annoyment
Horribleness,
Madness,
Anger,
Anger,
Anger.

Brodie Moir (7)
St Lawrence CE Primary School, Sevenoaks

Worry

Distressed,
A broken friendship,
Worried,
Under pressure,
Apprehensive,
Disturbed,
Tense, anxious,
Upset.
My life turns a bend.

Rory Mylroi (9)
St Lawrence CE Primary School, Sevenoaks

Scared

Shock,
Horror,
Tingling down my spine
The fear.

Afraid,
Haunted,
What will I do?
Fear strikes everywhere.

Tara Whitaker (10)
St Lawrence CE Primary School, Sevenoaks

Anger

A fierce, dark person
An angry, dark shadow
A horrible creature to the world
A dark, fierce figure
A bad, mean, selfish thing
An unkind bully
Infuriated
Anger.

Ben Thomson (7)
St Lawrence CE Primary School, Sevenoaks

Anger

A swirling pool of anger,
A dark soul lurking in my body,
My skin is glowing red,
A terrifying fire monster,
A volcano erupting
Anger strikes again
Anger.

Liam Shoulder (9)
St Lawrence CE Primary School, Sevenoaks

Armchair

Depressed, heavy-hearted
In my little armchair.
Children grow up
In my little armchair.
Years pass
In my little armchair.
Left behind
In my little armchair.

Korban Mullick (9)
St Lawrence CE Primary School, Sevenoaks

Anger

Fused up to everything you see,
Mad,
Infuriated,
So much fury you feel like breaking everything you see.
Bad-tempered
A fiery figure,
Annoyance,
Anger!

Sam Phillips (8)
St Lawrence CE Primary School, Sevenoaks

Anger

A red-hot flame, with a deep blood-red colour, spreads
through your body.
A race from Hell, a bitter bite on your soul.
Anger meets the mouth, loud shouts echo in the shadows.
One step back and Hell is at your back.
You turn off the light though a faint light is still on; a faint light of
anger.

Leia Whitaker (10)
St Lawrence CE Primary School, Sevenoaks

Furious

Rising rage,
A temper like a wolverine,
He was the boss of competitiveness.

The leader needed revenge,
He was furious!
Hot under the collar.

The chief got wrathful.

Mihran Choudhury (11)
St Lawrence CE Primary School, Sevenoaks

Anger

Deep, deep in your head is Anger
He is a blob of no help
He is your anger
Anger will burst out like a rocket with no warning.
Please keep him in your head not in your words
He will be no help to you
Anger!

Toby Kirkpatrick (8)
St Lawrence CE Primary School, Sevenoaks

Anger Awakens

Anger is no help,
My fists scrunching up,
My body heating up,
My face going red,
My skin catching fire,
Anger strikes again.

Wilf Wiles (9)
St Lawrence CE Primary School, Sevenoaks

Shocked

Earth-shattering, blasting cannons,
With noisy shells fighting at the enemy,
Shells as loud as a sonic boom.
Deafening, harsh-voiced rockets,
Screeching through the sky,
Everyone has shell shock.

Adam Reeve (9)
St Lawrence CE Primary School, Sevenoaks

The Scary Story

The sad and pensive man lost his job.
The sorrowful man hit his friend after a battle.
In the house it was dark.
The heavy-hearted woman lost her husband.
The upset man lost his keys.
Which vanished away, out of his hand.

Amir Mayow (10)
St Lawrence CE Primary School, Sevenoaks

Worry

Distress, worry, upset,
A disturbed, torn-apart friendship
A knock over
An overthrow
Worried for what is to come
Afraid, thinking about the past.

Joseph Sayers (10)
St Lawrence CE Primary School, Sevenoaks

A Poem Of Shock

Flabbergasted, dumbfounded, lost for words,
Overwhelmed by devastation,
Raving mad with panic.
Stress and adrenaline,
Nutty and depressed,
It was a disaster.

Freddie Rudd (9)
St Lawrence CE Primary School, Sevenoaks

Down In The Dumps!

A hopeless, careworn man
Walks along a windy road,
His name is Dan,
Dan's stressed, pained and gloomy
He is miserable,
And moody.

Sophie Jean Louise Bryer (11)
St Lawrence CE Primary School, Sevenoaks

Waiting For A Friend

Lonely, scared, afraid,
Watching people pass,
Playing happily,
With me
Alone,
Waiting for a friend.

Maisie Brooks (10)
St Lawrence CE Primary School, Sevenoaks

Joy

Happiness,
Joy took over sadness
His parents seemed to follow him,
The fear shadow dispersed as he thought about saving his brother,
Happiness filled his lungs,
Joy.

Oliver Philip Peter Lloyd (8)
St Lawrence CE Primary School, Sevenoaks

Anger

Devil's boiling brain,
Red, spiky hair
Boiling water flooding up,
Scattered people scared,
Fire spitting everywhere.

Rupert Dartnell (9)
St Lawrence CE Primary School, Sevenoaks

Anger

Beast
Exploding fire
Lost temper raging
Nasty, spiky
Anger.

Edward Mack (7)
St Lawrence CE Primary School, Sevenoaks

Shocked

Shocked, alarmed,
Nervous at the jangled nerves,
Everywhere noise,
Startled
Shell-shocked!

Amelia Violet McNeir (11)
St Lawrence CE Primary School, Sevenoaks

Heart-Warming Happiness

H appiness comes from the heart
A lways try to play your part
P eace is a part of happiness
P oints of view are always good
Y et making friends you always should.

Sofia Ferguson (7)
St Mary's & St Peter's CE Primary School, Teddington

A Mixture Of Emotions

I got out of bed,
Excitement was in my head,
The thought of seeing all my friends,
And telling them about my weekend.

I left the house with joyful swagger,
Smiling at everyone I see,
And feeling very happy.

After the usual assembly and lessons,
My cheerful feeling remained,
Until something happened at playtime,
And everything changed.

I was playing with a ball,
But someone changed all the rules.
I went to sit alone on a bench,
Feeling left out and upset,
Then I started to feel regret,

I wished I was with my friends having fun.
And not feeling cross with everyone,
My mood changed so fast,
And now I want to put it in the past.

Daisy McCutcheon (9)
St Mary's & St Peter's CE Primary School, Teddington

Always Shy!

I'm always sad, I'm always shy, I'm always nervous even to try.
I don't have fun with my friends even when there's nothing wrong.
Every day I get to play with no fun at all.
On my first day of school I cried and cried because I was so shy.
Since then I hated school,
Nothing could make it better except for being brave.
When we do class assemblies
I don't like being in them because you stand up in front of
lots of people.
I always turn blue in front of you because I'm shy.
Oh yes, I'm shy. I'll never be brave but I will try.

Inês Araujo (7)
St Mary's & St Peter's CE Primary School, Teddington

Fear Frights

Fear is a feeling that everyone hates
It is a door to terror and fright
Some panic in the day time
Whilst others at night
Creepy-crawlies, spiders, rats
Whatever causes you distress.
Creaky floorboards, howling winds
There's nothing you like less,
But when you're feeling anxious
Remember it's all in the mind
So take a deep breath and think of something kind!

Sasha Sylvester Bowles (9)
St Mary's & St Peter's CE Primary School, Teddington

One Of All

My eyes rolled back in my head,
I just wanted to be back in bed,
My sheets warm and cuddly, my face swarmed with glowing glee,
You couldn't know how much rest meant to me.

Smile on my face,
My nose in the air,
Chin held up high,
I was proud as a prancing panther, to be fair.

My legs were kicking back
As I started to scream.
I wouldn't be much use
In a friendly team.

A jubilant face
A warm, rose glow
If I was sad,
You'd never know.

A blue, glum grimace
A silent moan
Tears on my cheeks
A little groan.

My teeth were chattering,
Not because I was cold
I had a sneaky feeling I'd still be here
When I was very, very old.

A lump in my throat
My lips flaky and mouth dry
I couldn't even smile
If I'd wanted to try.

With plummeting heart and pounding ears,
My blood was pumping so I couldn't even hear.

Lila Johnson Roberts (8)
St Mary's & St Peter's CE Primary School, Teddington

Being Brave And Having A Go

I had an amazing holiday
On a trip to Disneyland,
Until we queued for a roller coaster,
A ride I couldn't stand.

'Be brave,' Mummy said, but my tummy was in knots
As we were about to get on the ride.
My hands were shaking rapidly
I wanted to go and hide.

We started slowly then plunged into darkness
Then upside down, spinning round the bend
Faster than a cheetah, screaming madly
I closed my eyes and wished it would end.

As we came out of the tunnel
My eyes were still shut tight
'Can we go on it again?' I laughed
It was really quite all right.

Isabel Caitlin Harper (8)
St Mary's & St Peter's CE Primary School, Teddington

Scary Sights

He's scratching at the door.
It may be a war.
I'll defeat you down.
And I'll have the crown.
Did you know that you are not real?
I'm really scared, I feel like I'm an eel.
I really need to hide.
If you wouldn't mind.
You have to die.
If you were kind, I would make you a pie.
Know that's all of it for today.
If you died, I would shout hooray!

Ava Rose (7)
St Mary's & St Peter's CE Primary School, Teddington

The Best Birthday!

I open my eyes
Hop out of bed
What a wonderful surprise!
Excitement is buzzing in my head
I can't wait!
It's going to be the biggest, best birthday
There'll be sweet scrumptious cake
And I'll make a wish
I am jumping to the clouds
I am so excited
Because when I get my gifts
I'll be so delighted!
The doorbell goes ring
Ding, dong, ding!
Starting from now
It's going be the best birthday ever.

Olivia Parker (8)
St Mary's & St Peter's CE Primary School, Teddington

Christmas Nerves!

I'm tucked up in bed with covers over my head,
Waiting for the thud of thick, black boots.
My heart is beating quickly, I'm feeling rather sickly
Waiting for the sound of Christmas suits.
Am I shaking with excitement?
Or shivering with fear?
How much longer will it be until he's actually here?
I want to hear the jingle but really I'm not sure.
Lying in my bed watching my bedroom door!
My eyes are feeling heavy, I really want to peep,
I can't stay awake, I just want to sleep, sleep, sleep...

It's the start of Christmas Day and actually it's turned out OK!
There was no need to fear and I'm full of Christmas cheer!

Ava Shore (8)
St Mary's & St Peter's CE Primary School, Teddington

Anger

Anger, the king of emotions,
Horrible and spiteful
He ruins all loving notions.
His heart is all stone cold.
Even though he's a terror to lives
He stands out fierce and bold.
Angry Anger's personality's so bad
I wonder, wonder why
We find this so sad.
Fearsome ire,
Like a fire.
Anger likes to scream and shout.
Please, oh, please, don't let him out!
Don't let him escape today.
Take a deep breath -
Blow him away.

Sophie-Zelda Marsh (8)
St Mary's & St Peter's CE Primary School, Teddington

Loneliness

Loneliness, a feeling that is really not a feeling,
It is a crying fit,
A circle of shame,
A bubble of depression,
A world of isolation,
A life of disappointment,
You're sitting alone on a wooden bench,
You're thinking of something no one else would,
You're someone only you can be,
A sad, mad, lonely person,
Your face as pale as a watery sun,
Your life as dead as a rotting corpse.
Loneliness.

Tess Bennett Jones (8)
St Mary's & St Peter's CE Primary School, Teddington

147

Dramatic Desolation!

Desolation is destruction and despair,
You are a bird close to death that once flew in the air.
You are trapped; you'll never be as before,
Happiness is in your life no more.
You are like a tree that's fallen in a storm,
You fear your heart will never be warm.
Desolation can be caused by a city tumbling down,
Or your friend deserting with their face in a frown.
So don't get yourself in such a state, or the world around you,
You will hate.

Megan Ferguson (10)
St Mary's & St Peter's CE Primary School, Teddington

The Excited Fish!

I am a fish called Splosh,
And I swim in my tank all day.
I feel bored and lonely.
No one to talk to or play with,
But one day in excitement I saw a person who said,
'Come with me to the river to meet some other fish.'
Oh happiness! I'm going to be free!
I met a really nice fish.
But I was the only fish who had rainbow patterns on my body.

Sophie Greenwood (7)
St Mary's & St Peter's CE Primary School, Teddington

When I Feel Joy

When I'm smiling I feel joy,
And spread it to every girl and boy.
When I'm in a show, I feel a perfect pro,
That makes me feel joy for everyone, even Roy.
It's nice to feel positive,
Especially with my family.
So let's spread joy around today,
Come on you, let's go and play!

Phoebe Tan (9)
St Mary's & St Peter's CE Primary School, Teddington

Excitement

You're excited when you're at a party.
You're excited when you're buying a new toy.
Excitement is a wonderful thing which makes people want to sing.
Excitement is a butterfly with gold, shiny wings like the rays
of the sun.
When you're excited your eyes shine with sapphires under the
moonlight.
That's what excitement is!

Kate Wilson (7)
St Mary's & St Peter's CE Primary School, Teddington

The Safety Of Love

Love is like a box
In the strongest of safes,
Where no anger, fear or hatred
Can ever, ever reach!

Ben Fine (8)
St Mary's & St Peter's CE Primary School, Teddington

Sadness

Sadness lives in the coldest places,
Where the penguins and polar bears lay,
But sometimes she moans without any sign,
Sometimes she can't run and hide.

Being called names, she's been kicked out of games,
These are the things that make sadness cry,
She will moan saying she wants to be alone.

Her face is blue,
Her skin is wet,
She is the saddest emotion around,
The emotions get annoyed,
They scream and run away,
She is the most annoying emotion in town.

The only way to stop her,
Is to smile and say hello,
Enormous smiles and glee,
Will make annoying Sadness flee.

Sadness' skin is blue,
She lives in the cottage where the penguins are found,
But hopefully now we won't see her again,
Now I have found a new friend.

Maisie Kneller (9)
St Mary's Catholic Primary School, London

Height

Up in my harness,
Safe but alone,
I wonder if anybody is above or below,
I feel like I am going to be sick,
Oh no,
Then there is a spider there,
I flick and I hit but luck is found.
So for the first time I freeze.

I am so scared that I'll fall,
Just looking down,
Shall I turn my head around,
So I look up at the view,
I think what a lovely day too.

I try to take my harness off,
So I smash and bang around,
I get my harness off,
And climb towards the ground.
I fall and fall,
Landing with a thud
I am finally back down.

Lucas Magill (8)
St Mary's Catholic Primary School, London

Untitled

Happy, I am so happy. I just can't wait,
I want to inflate.
Don't feel glum, don't feel dumb,
Just be happy, happy, happy.

Anger makes people mad and makes people sad.
Anger says everyone's not going to get something right,
Then makes it into a fight.
He goes under the ground all around.

Conor Watkins (7)
St Mary's Catholic Primary School, London

151

The Dentist

The deafening sound runs through my ears,
The mean cackle makes me jump in fright,
Leaning back on the leather chair, the light shining in my eye,
He gets his drill out of his box . . .
Fear is running down my spine.

I can hear him coming to the door,
I'm screaming but no one can hear,
He's getting closer, I'm going to run.
But he's already here . . .
Fear is running down my spine.

I'm going to die, I'm going to die,
He's getting out his tweezers,
He says, 'Open wide,'
Fear is running down my spine,

He's going to kill me in a click,
I hope he's extra quick,
He'll pull my teeth out through my chin.
Fear is running down my spine for the last time . . .
It's done and over, it hurts no more.

JJ John Howe (8)
St Mary's Catholic Primary School, London

Mathster

When I come through the gate my worry monster is waiting for me.
He thinks, *where is he? I must get into his bag,*
I go to school,
I don't feel confident because my monster makes me look like a fool.

I feel upset when I don't get ten out of ten.
Usually I feel better than then.
I feel like a loser when I don't get a good score.
He gets me thinking I want to be good at the activity.
But I take a breath and with the speed of a click he's vanished.

Christian Andrew (8)
St Mary's Catholic Primary School, London

Danger

Danger follows me downstairs,
A glass of overflowing water shakes,
But I hear a sound so familiar,
Bubbling burning from the stone fireplace.

Danger is near,
It is too tempting for me,
It is red, yellow and orange as far as the eye can see,
It is like it is calling my name,
As I close my eyes and rub them,
But when I open them it is all the same.

Danger is close, my heart is racing,
All I can hear is noises,
A dark door has opened as black as night,
With cobwebs in the corners and spiders on the floor.

Danger wants to get me,
I can feel it in my bones,
Then Dad comes down to turn the fire off,
It's bedtime now, lights go off,
But I still think there are spirits.

Hannah Ivy Tribe (9)
St Mary's Catholic Primary School, London

Angry, Happy, Funny

When I am angry I stamp my feet and scream.
It is so loud, no one stands round me!

When I am happy I make people joyful.
It is hard work being happy but it is making people joyful.

I am funny, I love my mummy,
I think my mummy is funny too.

I am funny, I am angry, I am happy.
No matter who you are, be the way you are.

Lucy Rodney (7)
St Mary's Catholic Primary School, London

Joy

Joy lives in the high blue heavens,
She is kind and loving, she is never in the way,
You can trust her every day and she'll hold you tight.
Joy will help you through your fears,
Joy will be your bubble
She'll never let you go,
Even in the night,
She'll hold you tight.

She'll make you happy like the day,
She'll make you dance around,
She'll make you smile like the sun,
The whole day through,
When it's over she'll say, 'I held you tight.'

When it's night,
She'll say goodnight,
She'll give you a teddy,
And hold you tight.

In the morning she says, 'Hello'
Then she says, 'I held you tight.'

Teri Mya Moniz (9)
St Mary's Catholic Primary School, London

My Worry Monster, Spellings

When I put my pencil down he is already there.
I try to push him away but he just stays there.
I tried to play but he just stayed.
I can't even sleep because he is always saying,
'You are going to get it wrong.'

The next day I took a deep breath.
and I pushed him away
Then I was always happy from that day on.

Isabella Maria Kolnikaj (8)
St Mary's Catholic Primary School, London

Darkness

When you're in the dark,
You never know what's lurking there,
You want to get to sleep,
But you never want to close your eyes.

They're probably under the bed,
But you're too petrified to look,
Or they could be in a cagey corridor,
Or they could be right next to your terrified face.

You might be hearing horrifying noises,
Or it might just be your creepy mum,
You finally get to sleep,
Until your uncontrollable cats start to fight.

You wake up again too early in the morning,
You can't get to sleep until your mum sings you a lullaby,
You wake up for it to be just a bad dream.

When you open the window like it is a door to freedom,
You realise it wasn't a dream,
But it was an extremely bad day.

Tristan Rhys Brooker (9)
St Mary's Catholic Primary School, London

Sadness

Sadness is the blue sky
Sadness is the blue tears that run down her blue top all the
way to her feet,
It's rain that falls onto the umbrella and splashes onto her
cold blue back.
Sadness is the blue wind, the blue earth, her blue zigzaggy jumper,
Her blue shoes and her blue long hair.
Sadness makes me lonely,
Sadness makes me sad,
But when joy comes around, she builds a smile on my face again.

Alissa April Brooker (7)
St Mary's Catholic Primary School, London

Shadows

Every night I wait in fright for it to jump out at me.
It's as scary as can be,
It glares at me with a frightful look,
It feels as scary as reading a scary book.

I'm sleeping very tight,
But every night,
I'm scared with so much fright.
It freaks me out every night.
With shadows I don't even like.

It's nearly light,
But I jump with fright,
Then the tremendous light comes out,
I'm not scared anymore.

I don't have to fear anymore.
I will deal with this by steering my path away.
I will deal with this by not looking anyway.
I'm not scared of you!
I'm not afraid of shadows!

Eva Noakes (7)
St Mary's Catholic Primary School, London

People Get Hurt

Every day he waits at the gate,
With a grin on his face.
Every day I'm playing with my mates,
And he says that's great.
Every day I'm in class with my mates,
He trips them up with the invisible weights.
He's on my back saying, 'Thanks for that, the weight was great!'
He is saying, 'I gave him the weights.'
I start being sad.
I trip them up and then fall on the invisible weights.

Lucas Brian Khan (8)
St Mary's Catholic Primary School, London

Fear Of The Dentist!

Fear is hidden all over me
Even in the deepest corners of my body,
He lurks around my mind
When I go to the dentist,
As I hop into the car Fear races through my head,
Vrummm the silver car starts
Fear sits in my brain shivering.

In the waiting room it's just me and Fear,
Hearing all the screams coming from somewhere near,
I slowly shuffle my feet getting nearer to the dentist.

When I get in the room
My mummy looks worried,
The dentist has a drill as threatening as a chainsaw,
The metal tools clatter against my teeth,
Cling, clang,
And the dentist carries on,
After a minute all the pain is gone.
The dentist is amazing.

Emilie Abbott (9)
St Mary's Catholic Primary School, London

Darkness

The light goes out
My worry begins to set in
I hoar footsteps creaking, stomping, cracking in complete darkness.

Shadows come from under the bed
But it is all in my head
But nothing is there.

Tossing and turning
I hear noises all around
My heart beats
I realise it was the neighbour's pet growling in the dark.

Calum Justice (9)
St Mary's Catholic Primary School, London

Birthday

It comes every year,
Surprised like a new day,
In the month called May,
And in that month it's my birthday.

Having fun with my family and friends,
Playing and playing all night long,
I smell delicious chocolate all around,
The lights turn off,
Starting a peaceful party like a bird's nest;
Came along with a song.

Singing and dancing,
Talking and laughing,
Nobody knows how long,
Eating chocolate cake but it tastes horribly wrong

It is always a surprise,
What I get for my birthday,
The excitement is just unbearable.

Isabelle Liu (8)
St Mary's Catholic Primary School, London

Nightmare With School

Every Monday a monster is in a playground.
When I go in to school
I feel like I'm getting it wrong.
But then I kick the monster and put it in the toilet.
Every Tuesday it comes back watching at the gate.
It makes me late.
On Wednesday I put him away.
So I can be nice to my friends at play.
I work hard all day.
I will not let school worry me.
The monster will never defeat me.

Dylan Ryan (7)
St Mary's Catholic Primary School, London

Darkness

Shadows creep into my room, not letting me hide,
I'm alone, I hear footsteps as light as a mouse,
Talking dolls, ghosts, clowns,
They're the ones that scare me the most

Soon, in each corner are my nightmares.
I start to sweat and get hot,
I think about what's under my bed.
Not knowing.

I hear little steps and scary laughs coming to my door,
Squeak, squeak, he comes in
As quick as thunder he comes onto my bed
The only reason they come is for me,
This one is my worst monster, it scares me the most.

I hear footsteps again coming in,
Please don't say it's another monster,
Light turns on, it comes again.
Saving me, my mum, she protects me the most.

Rory O'Neill (9)
St Mary's Catholic Primary School, London

Pip The Friendship Breaker!

Pip is a worry monster wandering about,
Pip is a loud monster very likely to shout!
Every break time and lunchtime he is waiting for me,
But he is probably as small as a pea.

Pip is the friendship breaker,
But he is not a good baker!
I always dread playtime,
When he steals the friends of mine.

But I pick him up and flick him away,
And now he knows he has to pay!

Ciarcey McMorrow (7)
St Mary's Catholic Primary School, London

Danger

I turn the light off
I hear deep breathing like danger is coming towards me,
A haunted ghost is sneaking up the crackling stairs,
I race to a handy hiding hole.

The hideous witch walks away,
But danger is near,
I can hear it through my senses,
I stride downstairs.

I creep into the kitchen,
Not making the smallest sound
I hear a sound and turn around,
My mum is here,
They take the monster away.

My worry is blown away
My happiness is back to stay.

Ryan Michael John Hackett (8)
St Mary's Catholic Primary School, London

Times Tables

I walked in school.
I played with my friends, then the bell rang.
We hurried into the classroom,
Our teacher gave us a times table test
Timesy was saying, 'You're going to get it wrong!'
She liked to annoy me,
So I flicked her off my back.
Then the teacher said, 'We're going to mark.'
I was really worried but I got them all right.

I always come to school
Timesy is waiting every Friday.
She always worries me then the spelling test comes.
I'm even more worried than ever.

Lily Murray (7)
St Mary's Catholic Primary School, London

Darkness

When I'm alone a monster comes,
I run down the stairs in a flash,
Tiptoeing through the hallway,
Creeping behind me . . . there he is,

My body is shaking, I am petrified,
Unknown shadows dancing,
Brain racing, searching for a trapdoor,
Fear flashing everywhere in the room.

Feeling super scared and alone,
Worrying what's hiding in the cupboard,
Worrying what's hiding under the bed,
Worrying what's hiding behind the door.

The light turns on and nothing is there,
My worry monster is gone.
Hopefully until tomorrow night.

Keira Martin (9)
St Mary's Catholic Primary School, London

Untitled

Every Friday he's waiting at the gate with a devilish scary glare on his face.
When I got outside for break time he was already out there
To tell me I was going to get them wrong.
I got back into class and it was time for our spelling test.
He was worrying me right there.
I wrote them down and got them all right but he's always there for next time.
The next day I tried to blow him away but he just didn't go away.
I tried and tried but he just stayed in his place.
But one day I scared him away
By putting my monster costume on and he ran away.
Then he never came back again.

Christianna Davies
St Mary's Catholic Primary School, London

Darkness

It comes every summer when I am alone,
Slowly creeps within the unknown shadows,
It watches my every move,
When it's night it comes to scare me,
Leaving me nowhere to hide.

My face is getting sweaty like the deep blue sea.
The creatures are dancing across to me,
My mind escaping for a trapdoor.

Sprinting as quickly as lightning to my covers,
Worried what's in the cupboard,
Monsters, witches and living dolls,
Are these creatures ever going to leave me alone?

I hear creaking from outside,
Heart beating, fist pounding, eyes shut no more
I have beaten my worry monster again.

Ethan Elton (8)
St Mary's Catholic Primary School, London

My Worry Monster

I'm scared of clowns, I don't know how they're always in my head.
It's creepy like the BFG.
It's hard to see, he's very scary.

When I'm sleepy he shouts at me
I'm scared to death.
I try to be happy but I fail.
It's so hard to see how creepy they can be,
Please go away.

I'll breathe three times,
I'll blow him off,
He'll never be there,
Now I'm happy he's not snappy.

Jamie Roberts (7)
St Mary's Catholic Primary School, London

Darkness

I'm in a gloomy corridor,
With no escape doors, every exit is locked,
Ready to scream, doors flying open,
My mind is twirling.

Screech in the corners,
Lockers with glass inside,
Looking for an escape route
Why me?

Footsteps racing behind me,
Dogs miaowing, cats howling, owls roaring,
Why me? Can't it be someone else,
Is it true or just a frightening dream.
What emotion am I?

Answer: Fear.

John Taylor (9)
St Mary's Catholic Primary School, London

Worry

It lives in my head,
Whispering, 'Danger, danger . . .'
When there are tests, it tells me that I'm wrong,
This has been going like that far too long.

It is there when I look for my things.
Where did they go? Where did they go?
Does it hide them from me?
Maybe. I don't know.

I know I can stop it.
By doing my best,
When I feel great, it quickly runs away.
Then calm and joy returns,
Hopefully to stay.

Alba Huba (8)
St Mary's Catholic Primary School, London

Joy, Anger And Love

Joy lives high in the clouds of your heart,
Living in a house of clouds,
Everyone likes her kind and caring nature,
Like the sun she radiates warmth, hope and love.

Anger is the fiercest emotion of all,
He is the brother of fear,
His hobby is to strike panic into the hearts of everyone.
He lives in the tip top branches of the creator's tree.

Love is the strongest emotion of all,
It's what people think when they say nothing at all.
She makes your heart sing, like a majestic opera,
She makes you feel joyful, like parents seeing their newborn baby,
She acts like a friend.
Filling everybody with hope and a smile.

Aidan Thomas Byrne (9)
St Mary's Catholic Primary School, London

The Roller Coaster

Every day this happens, a roller coaster ride,
Zooming up and down the tracks,
Terrible butterflies surround in my stomach,
On the roller coaster I am scared but excited,
The roller coaster is rapidly coming down like a speedy bullet.
I am so scared.

There are loops coming up, I freeze with delight,
I hear sparks on the roller coaster,
It is like fire at night.

The ride is finally over,
My head is spinning,
My heart is beating fast,
My hands are shaking
But I'm safe off the ride.

Nina Brewer (9)
St Mary's Catholic Primary School, London

Anger

He lives in sight, his name is Anger,
Every night he climbs the walls,
Anger is very mad,
I have never seen him not be bad.

Anger is as mean as a bully,
He reminds me of robbers or danger,
Anger is as scary as a horror movie,
He even ruined something of beauty.

But one night my heart stopped beating,
I saw Anger sleeping,
Anger was deadly red,
That's a colour of a flame.

Bradley Gell (9)
St Mary's Catholic Primary School, London

Darkness

Every night when I'm alone,
I see a shadow from down below,
My heart is racing like a train,
I hope I won't see it again.

My fist is clenching,
I don't know what to do,
Then I hear a crash,
And I think I have to make a move.

I am dripping with sweat,
And I feel all wet,
Then it fades away,
I have beaten my worry monster again.

Isabel Willson (9)
St Mary's Catholic Primary School, London

Darkness

When night falls I am very alone,
A shadow is rattling in my bones,
Creeping up the stairs, past the corridor,
Wanting to hide under the floor.

My blood shivers and my blood's flowing faster,
I am in the darkness, this is a disaster,
I think the monsters have returned,
They can't do this they have to learn.

They are probably just waiting for me,
In my mind I need a special key,
But in come my parents bringing a night light,
The darkness is gone, so is my fright.

Edward Bines (8)
St Mary's Catholic Primary School, London

Stressing Out

Sometimes I stress, I stress over silly things that the awful day brings.
But you can stress about choking but please no poking.
Don't have violence, just be silence.
So one day I went to school and I broke the rule.

I was stressed so I made a mess.
I went to lunch and had a munch
My stress monster was sitting next to me and then I
bumped my knee.
'Ouch! I think I need to sit on a couch.'
Then I had a huge slurp and then came a huge burp.
I told my monster to go away.
I took a breath and blew until she turned into stew.

Isabella Hilda Morant (8)
St Mary's Catholic Primary School, London

My Worry Shadows

Every night my worry monster waits at my bedroom door.
When I get to the door he jumps on the floor.
He tickles me and I look at the floor and I see him looking
straight at me.

Then he whispers in my ear.
Shadow
But I say no in my brain
Shadow
But I say no in my brain
Noooooo!
But when I look at him I take three deep breaths then I feel much
better.

Maisie Howard (7)
St Mary's Catholic Primary School, London

The Times Table Monster

Every Friday I wait at the gate for my mate.
But Molly is watching me like a hawk.
Even when I go for a walk.

Every Friday when I'm taking a test, she never has a rest.
Taking the Mick, I'll kick and flick.
She never stops, 'You got it wrong.'

One day I was tough I thought what to do
I took a deep breath and *whoof!* I blew.
She was gone!

Aisling Byrne (7)
St Mary's Catholic Primary School, London

Nervousness

My hands are sweaty, I feel like a yeti.
I am baked like a hot cross bun.

I don't want to run I want to be good.
But I can't, but I could,
I still want to be good!

I don't know what to do?

I feel like I am going to be sick!

Sofia Ramirez Canessa (8)
St Mary's Catholic Primary School, London

Joy

Joy is happiness inside you and me and it always will be.
Joy is friendship deep down and it will always be around.
Joy is fun, better than the sun.
Joy is dreams floating around beams
Joy is a bubble floating around Mildred Hubble,
Joy is magic running through the wand.
Joy is the sound of a baby's first word.
Joy is the sound of my cousin laughing.

Isla Joy Ladbury (7)
St Mary's Catholic Primary School, London

Timey The Times Table Monster

Timey is my worry monster, he's waiting at the gate for me
and my mates.
When I am doing a test of times tables he's making me stressed.
He's whispering in my ear, he says I've got it wrong.
I get ten out of ten then he crawls in my hair.
I take three deep breaths and in a flash he is gone in the
mist of nowhere.

Hannah Walker (8)
St Mary's Catholic Primary School, London

The Break-Up Bully

Any random day Hannah and I break up.
It's getting on my nerves now, I've just had enough!
He clings on my back and I pull on my school hat over my ears so I
don't hear him.
He waits for me at the gate, he waits at the class door,
He even waits for me when I'm with my mate!
The very next day I blew him away and he never came back again.

Annabelle Epsley (8)
St Mary's Catholic Primary School, London

My Happy Monster

When I'm sad or scared or stressed,
Happy comes and cheers me up.
On Friday it's my spelling test,
He hops onto my shoulder and I smile,
When it's group three he tells me all the spellings.
When I get home he says, 'I made a few mistakes.'
And I say, 'Everyone makes mistakes and you're still my best mate.'

Liliana Wieleba (8)
St Mary's Catholic Primary School, London

Sadness

She makes me feel that I have no friends in the world and it is just me
all alone.
She smells like salty tears stolen from a lost angel.
When I touch her she is wet from her falling heartbreak.
She tastes forgotten and of all the things I do not like.
She has foggy glasses, her skin is blue and her hair is like ice.

Abigail Sugrue (9)
St Mary's Catholic Primary School, London

My Worry Monster

Every Friday morning he's waiting at the gate.
He's even there at break time when I'm playing with my mates.
And then when I am marking he's whispering in my ear.
'You're going to get it wrong,' he says, I just don't want to hear.
And when I get ten out of ten I really feel like laughing.
But when next Friday comes around he worries me again!

Lucas Corbett Cumberbatch
St Mary's Catholic Primary School, London

Love Is Hard To Find!

Love is hard to find.
It's not just round the corridor.
You can't bump into someone and have true love.
I had it once but lost it twice.
There are so many words to describe:
How beautiful he is.
He's as pretty as a puppy just born.
His eyes glisten in the distance.
He's the one for me, he's the one for me.
I love him, I like him, I love him, I like him.
Love is hard to find.

LouLou Dolaghan (9)
Shoreham Beach Primary School, Shoreham-By-Sea

Maths In Space

Your teacher explains what's happening to you
But you're really dreaming about what you could do.

Your teacher is talking about maths and sums
But in your mind you're a bee singing hums.

You're a million miles up in outer space
On the back of an alien in an alien race.

You're on a unicorn, flying high
Terrifically soaring through the sky.

Your head lays gently in your hand
And your mouth is not as dry as sand.

You stare at the teacher for a moment or two
And then build rocket boosters on an enormous shoe.

You shoot underground
And have a good look around,
Loads of worms and moles
And thousands upon thousands of holes.

Suddenly the teacher says your name
You suddenly feel a lot of shame.

She asks what is $6+3$
You wish you were still a bumblebee.

You decide to go with a casual 'err!'
And then another kid answers, ending 'Duh!'

All of a sudden you feel more shame
You imagine yourself as a lion with a mane.

You terrify a hen prowling about
Then turn into a plaice and swim with trout.

You bite your fingernail
As you think of a snail

Your boring class then happily ends
Hoopy, doopy, mega, loopy, bubble, bends!

Annabel Rose Tredgold (10)
Shoreham Beach Primary School, Shoreham-By-Sea

My Poem

Happy but then sad
Tall but then small
Crazy but then lazy
Lazy but then crazy
Night but then bright
Bright but then night
Sad but then happy
Small but then tall
Hall feeling cool
Hands high on the wall
Shopping at the mall
Shopkins in my bag
Happy but then sad
Weather is looking bad
Windows on the bus
People making a fuss
Looking at me
I'm not sad
I'm happy, I'm free.

Danielle Ancell (8)
Shoreham Beach Primary School, Shoreham-By-Sea

Untitled

My fear is a person whose shadow is always next to mine.
It's almost like he wants to be there,
He wants to make you feel the way he does: full of fear!
He follows you everywhere.
He places a snake bite in your throat.
Your throat goes all dry leaving you speechless.
He will never leave.
So my message is to have hope.

Ivy Figari (9)
Shoreham Beach Primary School, Shoreham-By-Sea

Sluggy Feelings

I'm just a slug
People throw me down the plug,
They call me disgusting,
But my name is Justin.

They chuck me in the bin,
Like a dirty old thing,
With the old potato peelings,
That hurts my feelings.

This makes me sad,
People are bad.
And that pesky robin,
It leaves me sobbin'!

But, I've had enough of all this.
I'm happy to be me.
So I'm going to live in a tree,
And eat kiwi!

Josh Owens (10)
Shoreham Beach Primary School, Shoreham-By-Sea

Anger

A nger is a very hard emotion to get out of.
N obody can get you out of your anger stage.
G ood that no one wants to get me more angry.
E ventually I calm down.
R egret is the hardest thing to feel.

Coco Jalloh (10)
Shoreham Beach Primary School, Shoreham-By-Sea

Woohoo! I've Won!

As they announce my name my heart skips a beat
Then I trudge up to the platform, I can't feel my feet!
I see everybody staring, then realise what I've done.
I look at everyone as they start to clap, wait a minute, I've won!
Half of my mouth twitches upwards and then I jump with glee.
And everyone gasps and stares at the shiny, gold medal
handed to me.
I feel so proud as everyone starts chanting.
I'm number one, all of my friends look happy for me,
especially my mum!
As I walk through the cheering crowd, I hold my head up high!
This is such an amazing experience my oh my!

Libby Ayres (9)
Shoreham Beach Primary School, Shoreham-By-Sea

Big Changes

New teachers, different ways
I can't say a single phrase.
Sad, anxious, worried, scared.
I entered the classroom, and everyone stared.
New school, stuck here
Where is home, is it near?
I want to go back, and see my friends
Seems like school will never end.
Getting better, getting good
Things make memories where I once stood.
Feeling happy, feeling strong
School hours don't seem so long.
I feel confident, I can speak out loud
Being in the new school, makes me proud.

Anouk Awen Parker-Tregoat (8)
Shoreham Beach Primary School, Shoreham-By-Sea

175

Happy With Excitement

I was so happy
I could feel my heart about to burst with excitement.
My hands were shaking frantically.
I could feel a screech of excitement popping up my throat.

Ellie Ballard (9)
Shoreham Beach Primary School, Shoreham-By-Sea

Rainbow, Rainbow

Rainbow, rainbow in the sky,
How I like to see you in the corner of my eye.
Rainbow, rainbow on the ground,
When I find your treasure,
I will feel proud.
Rainbow, rainbow, you're everywhere.
Rainbow, rainbow,
Raindrops are your tears.
Rainbow, rainbow,
Some people call them fears.

Charlotte Bibi Uddin (7)
Wonersh & Shamley Green Primary School, Guildford

Happiness In My Home

In the brambles
Between the thorns,
Running back home,
Home sweet home.
Through the cat flap,
Squeeze past the door,
Past the kitchen, along the corridor,
Push the door open.
Spot my friend,
Overjoyed to see them,
Want to snuggle up,
I hear my name,
'Seraphoena'
Run past the table,
Jump onto the couch,
Sit down,
Snuggle up,
Get stroked.
Happy as can be,
I am now free,
With my owner,
Who loves me for me,
I can rest now,
Feeling the heat of the fire.
Elated and calm,
Joyful and happy,
Back home,
All safe and sound.

**Isabelle Bouette, Jessica Wron, Eva Meakin,
William Holmes & Rory Kenyon (9)**
Wonersh & Shamley Green Primary School, Guildford

There's A Monster Under My Bed?

There's a monster under my bed
Scaring me at night
Can't go to bed
There's a monster under my bed
Monsters are lurking
Petrifying me like jumping off a high gargantuan cliff.
My blood-curdling rapidly
Breath panting like a dog chasing a cat.

There's a monster under my bed
Messing with my head
Fed up of being scared
I say to myself in my head
Over the bed I go
Bending down low
What do you think I spy?
A menacing monster's eye.

Seeing his ugly face
Makes my heart race
Runs out onto the floor
Then quickly out of my door
When I see him run
My troubles over and done.
At last I can go to bed
There's no monster under my bed.

Sujeen Thapa (10)
Wonersh & Shamley Green Primary School, Guildford

Angry In A Cave

I was angry at a time
It was scary but this feeling was all mine.
I was surrounded by flames
I didn't want to play any games.
Then I found my feeling
And that's what was stealing
All the wonder and light.
When the moon was high in the night
I found an anger stone and it meant I wasn't alone,
I hugged it like a baby blue tit, then I was happy.

Annabel Lucy Bulley (7)
Wonersh & Shamley Green Primary School, Guildford

Young**Writers**

Est.1991

Young Writers Information

We hope you have enjoyed reading this book – and that you will continue to in the coming years.

If you're a young writer who enjoys reading and creative writing, or the parent of an enthusiastic poet or story writer, do visit our website www.youngwriters.co.uk. Here you will find free competitions, workshops and games, as well as recommended reads, a poetry glossary and our blog.

If you would like to order further copies of this book, or any of our other titles, then please give us a call or visit **www.youngwriters.co.uk.**

Young Writers
Remus House
Coltsfoot Drive
Peterborough
PE2 9BF
(01733) 890066 / 898110
info@youngwriters.co.uk